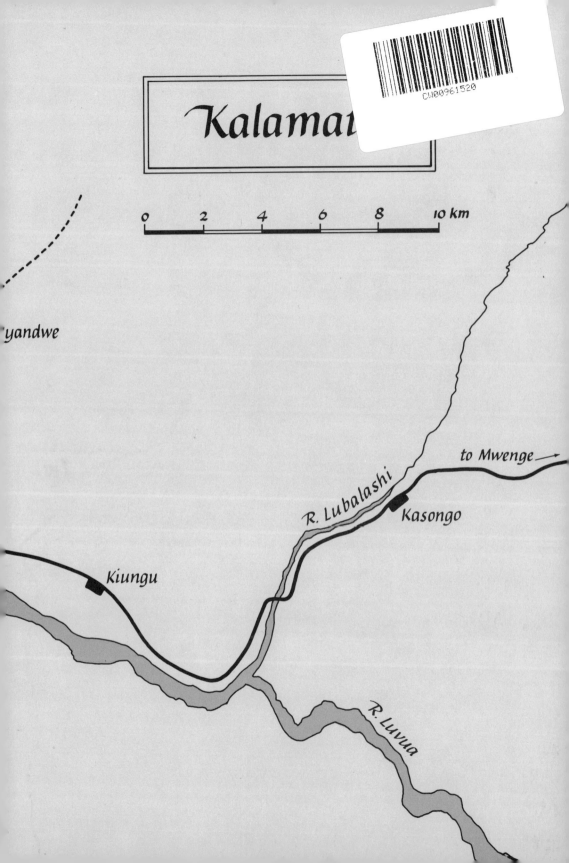

Kalamai

0   2   4   6   8   10 km

yandwe

to Mwenge →

R. Lubalashi

Kasongo

Kiungu

R. Luvua

THE ROAD TO KALAMATA

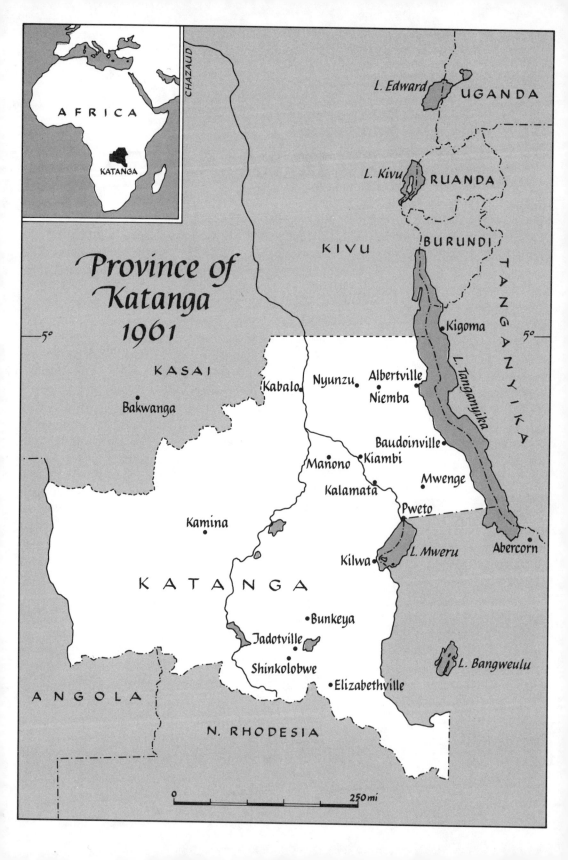

CHAZAUD

AFRICA

KATANGA

Province of
Katanga
1961

L. Edward

UGANDA

L. Kivu

RUANDA

BURUNDI

T A N G A N Y I K A

KIVU

Kigoma

L. Tanganyika

5°   5°

KASAI

Bakwanga

Kabalo

Nyunzu

Albertville

Niemba

Baudoinville

Kiambi

Manono

Mwenge

Kalamata

Kamina

Pweto

L. Mweru

Kilwa

Abercorn

K A T A N G A

Bunkeya

L. Bangweulu

Jadotville

Shinkolobwe

Elizabethville

ANGOLA

N. RHODESIA

0   250 mi

THE ROAD TO KALAMATA

A Congo Mercenary's Personal Memoir

MIKE HOARE

Leo Cooper

LONDON

First published 1989 by Leo Cooper

Leo Cooper is an independent imprint of the
Octopus Publishing Group, Michelin House,
81 Fulham Road, London SW3 6RB.

LONDON   MELBOURNE   AUCKLAND

ISBN 0–85052–2889
Printed in the United States of America

To my great American hero
Donald C. Rickard

Contents

Preface

TOWARD the end of 1960 and the beginning of 1961, Mr. Moise Tshombe, the president of the newly formed Independent State of Katanga, recruited a force of mercenary soldiers to help his fledgling army suppress a rebellion by the Baluba, one of the two great tribes in Katanga. While this was not the first time mercenary soldiers had been recruited for service in Africa in this century, it was nevertheless an event that was to cause considerable agitation at United Nations Headquarters and reams of comment in the world press.

In due course this initiative gave rise to an astonishing crop of highly imaginative stories about mercenary soldiering and mercenary soldiers, which were so far removed from the truth as to be laughable. I mention this in order that the reader may not be disappointed with this story, which sets out to be nothing more than an accurate if prosaic account of a tragic incident that took place during the Katanga campaign of 1961. If in the telling it robs mercenary soldiering of a little of its unexplained mystique, no great harm will be done.

Ten years after the Belgian Congo had become the Democratic Republic of the Congo, and later the Republic of Zaire, a large number of place names were altered in order to depict more accurately those places' indigenous origins. Leopoldville became Kinshasa, Elizabethville became Lubumbashi, Stanleyville became Kisangani, and so on. As the events in this story take place in the period just after independence I have retained the original colonial place names, which were then in use. The story is true and all the characters real live people. Here and there I have altered a name where it will save someone embarrassment.

1

4 Commando Musters

THE column had bogged down in the heart of enemy territory. The track had collapsed after days of torrential rains and more than twenty trucks had sunk into the mud up to their axles. We were surrounded by an army of unseen Baluba warriors, a tough and merciless foe. That day we had lost one of my men from a wound inflicted by a poisoned arrow. He had lasted less than sixty minutes and was our first casualty. Morale among my Katangese drivers was at rock bottom. My unit, 4 Commando, which was escorting the column, was on edge, several of the men down with malaria, the remainder near exhaustion from lack of sleep.

I often think back to that evening in that smoky, wet Baluba hut in an unnamed Baluba village in northern Katanga, with the rain pelting down and night falling fast, when I warned my officers of what might lie ahead. Our modern weapons and efficient logistical supply, I told them, did not of themselves ensure victory over a primitive, badly armed enemy. There were other potent factors to be taken into account. The harshness of the terrain and the tropical climate were among them. Then there was the abnormal character of our enemy. The fact that he tortured his prisoners ritually before killing them, that he used poisoned arrows and practiced cannibalism—these were tactical considerations they might not have encountered as soldiers elsewhere in the world. This was central Africa, not Europe. There was no Geneva convention here. Little did any of them think they would experience every one of the things I warned them about in the course of their service with 4 Commando.

I lay on the floor of the mud hut that night covered by a mosquito net and listened to the drumming of the incessant rain. Before dropping off to sleep, I thought back to that other world in which it had all begun.

A shabby Skymaster waited for us in a remote corner of the airfield as though glad to be out of the public eye. It looked tired and beat up. As we got nearer I could see traces of previous liveries on its tail plane, a sure sign it had changed hands more than a few times in the last twelve years. Just as I was beginning to feel a little uneasy I recognized the skipper, Captain Jack Malloch, a legendary figure in central African aviation. If he was the pilot I had nothing to worry about. Take Jack out of his blue serge uniform and his cap with the gold braid, put him in a white surplice and black cassock, and he would remind you of the most angelic bishop you had ever seen. He waved a hand in the direction of the sixty-three men who had sauntered across the tarmac with me to board the well-used DC 4.
"You in charge of this lot, Mike?" he asked with a smile.
"You could say that, Jack. How far is it anyway?"
"Just under a thousand miles. We overfly Bulawayo, Lake Kariba, and Lusaka."
"ETA Elizabethville?"
"Sixteen hundred hours—all being well."
"Any stops?"
"None scheduled." He laughed. "But you never know."
"Any weather?"
"Nothing we can't handle or go round. Box lunches on the back seat and brown paper bags for everyone." He grinned. "I think you may need them. Get 'em on board as quickly as you can, will you?" He clapped his hands. "OK boys, *andiamo.*"
Jack was not noted for his small talk. Two or three plain clothes security officials waved us good-bye in a friendly way, the doors were slammed, and the engines burst into life setting up that high-pitched vibration that always gets me worried. Jack nursed the old crate off the ground and then shaped a course due north for what used to be called darkest Africa. In places it still is, with good reason; but that was something I was going to find out for myself in the course of the next six months.
In the early stages of the flight I went round to introduce myself to the men and checked their names against the manifest Jack had given me. About twenty of them were South Africans, fifteen from

the U.K., and the rest Italians, Portuguese, and Rhodesians. The flight was uneventful as it turned out, but punctuated by moments of mild terror when we dropped heavily through thick black clouds. I noticed with some alarm that the wings of the DC 4 really did flap. I had often been told that Skymasters were famous for that engaging characteristic, but never really believed it until then.

Five hours later we were approaching the high plateau of Katanga, the watershed for two of the longest rivers in Africa, the Congo and the Zambezi. It was the time of the heavy summer rains and the land looked green, virile, and unruly. Below us unfolded a beautiful ranch-type country, unbelievably rich in mineral wealth of every description, but spectacularly so in copper. Five minutes from Elizabethville, the capital of Katanga, a single seater Fouga Magister jet-fighter screamed round us by way of formal inspection, just to remind us that the Independent State of Katanga was at war—internally with a recalcitrant tribe called the Baluba, and externally with the Democratic Republic of the Congo, from which Katanga had broken away, unilaterally, some nine months ago. We knew it already. After all, that was why we were here.

Some months prior to this Mr. Moise Tshombe, the president of the Independent State of Katanga, had decided to bolster up his newly raised defense forces by the recruitment of about seven hundred mercenary soldiers, the majority of whom would be Belgians and Frenchmen. By the end of February 1961 he had recruited five hundred men in Brussels and Paris and flown them out to Katanga. This recruitment in Europe rather than in Africa was a logical step to take as Belgium had been the former colonial power and French was the principal official language spoken throughout the Congo. The remaining two hundred men would come from Rhodesia and South Africa. The sixty-three men now arriving with me were the last of this intake.

At that time the new Katangese Army consisted of fifteen thousand recruits, plus about six hundred officers loaned by the Belgian Army for this special duty. The Belgians formed the staff, with their general headquarters, known as Etat Major, in Elizabethville. They had moved fast and in a few short weeks had established regimental depots and instructional cadres throughout the country. Within three months they were turning out officers, noncommisioned officers, and men for the new army at a reasonable standard. The proposed mercenary force recruited in South Africa and Rhodesia was not intended at this stage to be part of the Katangese Army proper but to serve as a form of gendarmerie whose duties would be of a paramilitary nature, in support of both the army and the police.

We taxied to a remote corner of the field and disembarked to be greeted by the Minister of Defense, Monsieur David Yav, and his Belgian Chef de Cabinet, Carlos Huyghe, a tall handsome man in his early thirties, the son of a former Governor General of the Belgian Congo. Immigration formalities were waived. We were hurried on to small buses driven by Belgian *sous-officiers* and whisked away in the direction of Jadotville, an important mining center about a hundred and fifty kilometers westward, and then a further thirty-five kilometers southwest of that to another mining center called Shinkolobwe. Shinko is famous for the copper mine that produced the uranium for the Los Alamos experiments, better known in history as the Manhattan Project, which resulted in the production of the world's first atom bombs back in 1945. We drew up at the cantonment, which appeared to be unoccupied. We were allotted villas previously lived in by Belgian technicians and their families, the majority of whom had left the Congo soon after it had been given its independence some nine months previously, or during the recent tribal fighting in Katanga.

The Belgian staff work was superb. In an hour we were fed and kitted out in the uniform of the Katangese Army. The only item of clothing that distinguished us from them and labeled us as gendarmerie was the bush hat, Australian type, which, while imparting a suitably romantic air, was to prove less than practical in the field. We listened to a short lecture by a Belgian officer on the military situation, embellished by some bloodcurdling comment on the nature of the enemy. This was designed, I felt sure, to disabuse the minds of some of us who might have thought we were going to be paid to lounge around in barracks. After a few drinks in the Mining Club canteen we got to know one another briefly and found our beds at a reasonable hour.

The following morning I examined the nominal roll. It showed a total strength of 121 officers and men. We were to be organized in two half companies, one of them to be led by Alistair Wicks, an ex–British Army officer, and the other by myself. I was to have overall command. This unit was not to be confused with a mercenary unit of about thirty men that had been raised a little earlier and called itself the White Legion, and sometimes the Compagnie Internationale when banded together with other Belgian mercenary units. Regrettably, at this moment the whole of the White Legion was languishing in a United Nations jail in Leopoldville, having been taken prisoner by Ethiopian troops of the U.N. peacekeeping force at Kabalo, a town in northern Katanga. But before their capture the Compagnie Internationale had distinguished itself in a fierce and decisive action against the Baluba at an important tin mining town named Manono, also toward the north of the country.

From the look of the names on the nominal roll it appeared the unit would be made up from about fifteen nationalities, the majority being Britons and South Africans. There were no Americans although a large number of Americans were sympathetic to Tshombe's cause and had made inquiries about enlistment in his forces. It was rumored at this time that Americans who enlisted for military service under a foreign flag would be committing an offense against the U.S. legal code punishable by confiscation of their U.S. passport. The belief in this draconian measure persisted for some years thereafter and deprived me of some excellent men later on when I commanded a unit of mercenary soldiers in the Congo known as 5 Commando. Later still it was found that there was no foundation in the law of the United States to substantiate that rumor.

At a glance I could see that we were going to have some problems with the organization. For a start there were far too many officers for a unit of 121 men. Officer rank had been conferred by Carlos Huyghe on an arbitrary basis grossly in excess of the fixed establishment for an independent company.

Most of the difficulty arose from a clause in our contract of engagement which stated that the volunteer was entitled to a rank one above that which he had held in his previous military service, full documentary proof being required to establish that, of course. A corporal would become a sergeant, a lieutenant a captain, and so on. A reasonable idea in theory, but there was no possibility of it working in practice. Alistair had been a captain. Was he now to be a commandant, the rank between captain and major equivalent to senior captain in the Katangese Army? I had been a major. Was I now to be a lieutenant colonel? *Malheureusement non*, they said. There was only one lieutenant colonel in the entire Katangese Army and he was the commander in chief, Lt. Col. Crèvecoeur, a Belgian. It did not worry any of us overmuch, and for my part I was quite content to accept the rank of captain provided only that I receive the appointment of commander of the unit now in formation. Rank, I thought in these circumstances, was not very important; one's appointment was the thing that mattered.

Another cause for concern was the stipulation made by the recruiting officer, one Captain Roddy Cargill, lately an officer in the British South African Police, that as there would be no time or facilities for any basic training all volunteers must be old soldiers who *had been in action.* This requirement, while highly desirable, was in fact impossible to fulfill, and led in due course to the ostentatious display of World War II and Korean War medal ribbons, bogus in many cases you may be sure, by all and sundry in an attempt to bolster their claims to previous military service.

But when you really get down to it, men who have actually been in action are much rarer than you might imagine. A travelogue of medal ribbons is no indication that their wearer has ever come under fire from the enemy. Vast numbers of soldiers serve their entire service honorably without ever hearing a shot fired in anger. It cannot be otherwise, and it is to some extent a question of proportion. During World War II it had taken twelve men to support one man in the firing line. In Korea this had risen to twenty-two, presumably the result of the advance in military technology and the advent of more sophisticated equipment. So by that reckoning men who had actually been in action were going to be quite hard to find.

To add to the general confusion on this point there was also some uncertainty as to what precisely was meant by "action." The terms "on active service" and "in action" are distinctive and not interchangeable, but nevertheless frequently confused in the civilian mind. "In action" in the military context means to be physically engaged in combat with the enemy; "on active service" means to be mobilized, ready to fight, serving under the colors but not actually fighting. In the present case it would be fair to say the majority of the volunteers had certainly been on active service, and all were certainly trained soldiers, but not very many of them had been in action.

A story from World War II illustrates the difference between the two terms succinctly. It was in Egypt, 1942. One summer's night Alexandria had been bombed very heavily by the Luftwaffe, resulting in appalling damage to that densely populated city. But even during the worst of the bombardment, Sister Street, the notorious brothel area, had been busy maintaining the morale of the troops, for such, I am happy to say, is the unflagging nature of this particular form of vice. Regrettably the red light district received several direct hits during prime time. The next morning unit padres were busy identifying the remains of soldiers killed in the raid. The question of classification then arose. How were the dead to be described in the casualty report: were they killed in action or killed on active service? The problem was resolved by the reverend gentlemen to everybody's satisfaction; those who were found with their trousers on were classified as "Killed on active service"; those who died with their trousers off were "Killed in action."

I introduced myself to the Company Sergeant Major, Stan Dowsey, and asked him to parade the men. CSM Dowsey had served in Burma during the war and we spoke briefly about Kohima and Imphal, where I had also served, checking on each other's credentials I suppose in the manner of old soldiers. He had been left behind by the White Legion when they moved out a few weeks before but he knew the ropes and the setup with the Belgians. He called the men to attention with a good word of command and that presence which is essential to the rank of sergeant major. The first thing that struck me was that the men were a mature lot and that their average age was probably nearer thirty-five than thirty. But this was not altogether surprising if they were to have seen service in World War II or Korea.

I inspected the men and had them call out their names as I came to them, a trick I had learned years before as a Second Lieutenant. This little dodge had always helped me fix a man's name and face in my mind. The second part of the trick is more difficult—to go round the ranks again, but this time you call out the men's names yourself from memory. This comes with practice. When you get it right it never fails to impress your men. Better than that it gives them to understand, very rightly, that you intend to know them as individuals. Getting to know your men is, may I say, the very first rule in man management and leadership. The second follows logically from that: get close to your men and care for them; a remote leader is an abomination.

I stopped opposite a rugged young Irishman.

"MacManus, Pathrick, sor! County Monaghan. R.U.R. Korea, sor!"

His turn out was immaculate.

"Royal Ulsters myself at one time," I said. "London Irish Rifles."

"Kirton, sir! South African Gymnasium. Cadet." A clean limbed blond giant, the epitome of a soldier.

"Hastie, Frank, sir! Glasgow. Royal Marines. Suez '56. Living in Salisbury now, sir."

"Rhodesian Army?"

"No, sir. Undertaker, sir." Some of the men tittered. The Sergeant Major silenced them with a glare.

I came to a fresh-faced man with a shock of red hair and pale blue eyes that seemed to look unnaturally into the middle distance.

"Auchterlonie, Alec, sir! Black Watch. Arrived yesterday from Scotland." The burr was delightful.

"Fit?"

"Yes, sir. Thank you, sir."

He was as straight as a wand, about thirty, tough and craggy. Good man, I thought. Can't have too many Celts. I love them. Sometimes a little hard to handle in barracks. The price one pays for fighting spirit I suppose, but worth it; always tremendous men in action.

"Do your best, Jock," I said and passed on to the next man.

To my astonishment Auchterlonie took a half pace forward, crashed his heel to the ground, and blurted out two lines of poetry in a heavy Scottish brogue while looking directly to his front in the best parade ground manner: But his Captain's hand on his shoulder smote: / Play up! Play up! and play the game!

I really didn't know what to say to that so I left it to the Sergeant Major to cope with the situation in the time-honored fashion.

"See me after parade, Auchterlonie!" said Stan. His tone indicated he wasn't going to stand any of that damned nonsense. That odd look in Auchterlonie's eyes disturbed me again, but I let it go. Clifton Chapel was, after all, a long, long way away.

"Kruger, sir, Henry. South African Infantry. They call me Errol Flynn." We all laughed but I could see why. He was a muscle man and as handsome as his namesake. I couldn't see him breaking many hearts around here and wondered why he had joined up.

At the end of the center rank was a small wiry man of about forty-five, maybe more. He looked hard as nails, his skin the color of beaten bronze, like an Alpine ski instructor. His flattened nose and battered ears told their story.

"MacKay, sir, Ted," he said, softly. "Middlesex Regiment. Regimental champion, bantamweight. Runner-up Southern Command."

"Fit, Mac?"

"Always, sir. It's my way of life." I could believe it.

Behind the rear rank, on his own, stood a huge man, resplendent in a kilt, a set of bagpipes tucked deftly under his arm. He must have been sixty if he was a day.

"Sandy King, sir! King's Liverpool Regiment. Eighth of foot!"

He wore a tam-o'-shanter—no Australian bush hat for him. His hair was basically gray but there were patches of black all over it where he had applied boot polish in an attempt to disguise it. Had he known me better he need not have bothered. For me there is no such thing as age, only the ability to do the job.

"Give us a tune then," I said. He piped up artfully "The Wearing of the Green." I stood the men easy while we heard him out. He was a good piper and the music stirred the blood.

"Storeman, sir?" suggested the Sergeant Major. I nodded. Sandy turned out to be a gem. He was a jack-of-all-trades. He could use a sewing machine, repair boots, mend anything, turn his hand to any job. But above all he was able to teach the younger men what soldiering was all about from his personal experiences and example. I was glad to have him in the unit.

"When I blow my whistle form up in a half circle around me and sit down." As I gave this old familiar command I felt I was putting the clock back fifteen years or more.

"Permission to smoke, sir?" asked Stan. I gave it. He barked out, "Smoke if you have them; those that haven't can go through the motions." The old corny jokes. Army life had changed little it seemed.

I have always believed that one of the most important things a leader must do is to talk to his men. I cannot think of anything as basic or as important as this for establishing that vital link which must exist between him as their leader and those he leads. By talking to his men, formally and informally, he lets them get to know what makes him tick. This is every bit as important as his getting to know them. There has to be a meeting of minds.

But communicating with one's men goes deeper than the mere passing on of orders. Soldiers must be made to feel that they are a vital part of their organization. They matter. If they are ignored and treated merely as numbers they will rapidly lose interest. To build on their natural enthusiasm a good leader has to capture their minds. He can do this only by talking to his men and impressing his personality on them. His style, diction, mannerisms, etc., are not so important as long as he gets his message across clearly, and if possible with a touch of humor. But he should keep what he has to say brief, prepare it carefully in advance, and use notes; and try not to be a bore or the end result will be worse than no communication at all.

Knowing the mind of your men is one of the arts of leadership. One of the great leaders of the First World War era was the Australian Field Marshal Lord Birdwood. He knew his men intimately, and they knew him. Birdwood always wore a monocle, something the down-to-earth diggers regarded as a bit of an affectation. On one occasion the Field Marshal inspected an Aussie battalion only to find every man had placed a piece of tin or a coin in his eye in an attempt to take the wine out of him. He went up and down the ranks without passing a single comment. Then he faced them. "OK, you bastards," he shouted, "you've had your fun—now let's see how many of you clever dicks can do this!" Taking out his monocle he threw it in the air and caught it in his eye! His men loved him.

I gave my new command the military and political situation in Katanga as I knew it and answered their questions. The majority of them were concerned in the main about the transfer of money to their wives and families. Incredibly some of them seemed to think that they would be paid in cash at the end of each week and were wondering how they could buy currency in order to send it home. Not one man asked how soon it might be before they would be sent into action. I gathered from that where their chief motivation lay.

Finally I told them we would get on well together if they remembered the golden rule: our unit is to be a fifty-fifty partnership; I give the orders and you obey them. This brought a laugh, but they got the message. I outlined the training program for the next few days, named the men who were to be their officers and NCOs, and dismissed them.

4 Commando had been born.

2

The Frightful Ones

I BEGAN by examining my command. We were intended to be an independent company and highly mobile. The war establishment had been designed on an elaborate scale, financial considerations being of secondary importance. This was not altogether surprising as we had been told that Union Minière du Haut Katanga, the giant mining conglomerate, was bankrolling the whole operation. Six jeeps, several one-ton and five-ton trucks, and three Volkswagen flatback troop carriers made up the unit transport. The stores were more than adequate and correct down to the last roll of Dannert wire. Communication within the unit was by PRC 9, the short-range backpack set used by the U.S. Army at that time. A powerful radio transmitter, capable of working several hundred kilometers to Etat Major in Elizabethville, would be provided as a rear link before we moved into the field.

The small arms were the same as those currently issued to NATO forces, and all were brand-new from Brussels. The basic arm was the FAL rifle, the 7.62 mm FN. Each platoon had three 7.62 mm MAG machine guns, belt fed. And section leaders and above were supplied, in addition, with the FN Browning 9 mm High Power pistol. One in four men was issued with an automatic weapon that was new to me, the Belgian 9 mm Vigneron M2 submachine gun. The weapon was light and handy and almost as good as the FN 9 mm UZI submachine gun, of which we had five. But the Vigneron had one weakness: the ejection opening cover was a bit tinny and had a tendency to snag on surrounding undergrowth when in the open position. The allotment of ball ammunition of all calibers, hand grenades, etc., was unbelievably generous and the practice ammunition almost limitless.

Our living conditions were excellent, the men being billeted four or five to a villa, which had running hot and cold water and electricity. A Belgian civilian ran the men's mess and in addition there was a well-stocked canteen. A swimming pool, a rifle range, spacious playing fields, and easy access to varied terrain made Shinko an ideal training camp. I don't think I have ever served in a better one.

The contract was for six months and covered all contingencies including compensation for loss of life, wounds, hospitalization, notification of next of kin, etc. We had to record whether we were left-handed or right-handed as this would effect our compensation if we lost a hand. One felt there was a competent legal mind behind the contract. The basic rate of pay was 150 U.S. dollars a month for a volunteer (the rank given to the private soldier or enlisted man) plus another 5 dollars a day danger pay, payable when a man was in an officially declared danger zone, making 300 dollars a month altogether. At that time 300 dollars would have been roughly twice as much as a qualified artisan could earn in his trade as a civilian in South Africa. Most men thought the rate of pay was reasonable having regard to the risk involved, although they had no means of assessing what that might be. As it turned out for most of them there would have been more danger crossing Fifth Avenue. My wages as a captain were roughly twice as much as a private soldier. There was also a daily ration allowance out of which we had to feed ourselves.

It soon became obvious to me that the health of my men would have to be my paramount consideration. Unfortunately, malignant malaria was an endemic disease in those parts of Katanga where we would be stationed, so a strict prophylactic drill would have to become part of our daily routine. Malaria was a killer. I found it strange that many of my men, particularly those from Europe, did not fully appreciate this. Many of them did not realize that malaria is Africa's greatest scourge and causes more deaths than all other diseases put together. Cerebral malaria, if we were unlucky enough to come across it, with its lethal fissiparous characteristic, was even more deadly. Not for nothing was it known as the four-day killer. We would have to take antimalaria pills every day without fail.

I was glad to find that our old friend mepochrine, the drug that turned us yellow in Burma and had us worried about our potency, and in some cases gave us jaundice, had been superseded. The pills now being issued were based on the drug camoquin. Having established that the health of each member of the unit was to be my chief concern I then turned to the nuts and bolts of training.

No directive was issued from above to guide me on this most important matter, nor was I given any indication of the manner in which my unit might be used. But after consultation at Etat Major with Belgian officers who had served with the Force Publique, the army of the Belgian Congo, I realized that a strictly European approach to the training of soldiers in the Katanga* would probably end in disaster. The basic advice these officers gave me, simply put, was "Stay alive to fight." The real enemies, they said, were the terrain, the climate, and disease. The human enemy, by comparison, was negligible. For every man killed or wounded by enemy action I would have twenty casualties from malaria, gangrenous infection, or venereal disease, some strains of which in this part of the world were resistant to all known forms of treatment and had the medicos completely baffled. A serious wound could turn gangrenous in four hours if left unattended, resulting certainly in the loss of a limb and in most cases in death. Tourniquets, the accepted practice where it was thought necessary to staunch the flow of blood, would in all probability hasten the onset of gangrene in these high temperatures. I decided that our training program must take these vital matters into consideration.

The basic training of an infantry soldier has remained surprisingly simple and constant over the centuries. I maintain that an infantryman's primary training requirements are, and in this order: to be supremely fit and hard, to be a master of his weapons, and to know how to dig. For modern warfare a soldier must not only be fit in body, he must also be abnormally hard in mind.

The fact that a man's mind requires hardening is a matter seldom addressed in the normal training of a soldier. The hardening of a man's mind may be a subject better suited to a psychiatrist than to a training officer, so the only comment I will offer here is to note that in my experience the barrack room atmosphere, the company and friendship of other hard men, severe physical hardships during

---

*Katanga, for no discernible reason, was usually referred to as *the* Katanga, rather like *the* Arakan in Burma. Maybe it was a literal translation of *le Katanga*.

training, singly and as a member of a team, all contribute to the required hardness of mind. In this connection it is often said that soldiering tends to brutalize. I would agree with that. I can't see how it can avoid doing so, given its ultimate object. But I don't think the condition is necessarily of a permanent nature. I prefer to think that the apparent shell of brutality is a temporary protection for the more sensitive ego lying just beneath the surface. One thing is certain, the soldier of today must find ways to harden his mind long before he is committed to action if he is to protect it against the horrors of modern warfare.

The infantryman's need for proficiency in weaponry is self-evident. That proficiency should include the stripping and firing of all weapons used by his immediate enemy as these can become a vital source of armament to him. I wonder how many soldiers of today could strip a Vickers machine gun if they were lucky enough to capture one. Yet this ubiquitous weapon, of which there must be many thousands extant in theaters of war all over the world, continues to pop up in the most unlikely places.

And as for digging, let those who may question the requirement recall Erich Remarque's famous passage in *All Quiet on the Western Front*:

> To no man does the earth mean so much as to the soldier. When he presses himself down upon her long and powerfully, when he buries his face and his limbs deep in her from the fear of death by shell-fire, then she is his only friend, his brother, his mother; he stifles his terror and his cries in her silence and her security; she shelters him and releases him for ten seconds to live, to run, ten seconds of life; receives him again and often for ever.

It takes very little exposure to the terror of a bombardment by mortar fire, or worse still accurate shell fire, to make one appreciate the truth of those remarks. There is no comfort like Mother Earth. I recall vividly at Kohima during the Burma campaign seeing men digging with spoons to get some cover when caught out in the open during a Japanese mortar attack. I also remember visiting the trenches made by the 2nd Battalion Royal Welch Fusiliers a few days later, and marveling at the dugouts, positive homes, created by those soldiers who had been, as most of them were, Welsh coal miners. I realized then that there is a soldierly art to be learned concerning the homely spade, the practice of which can save one's life. It was an art perfected by the Japanese soldier in the construction of his many-entranced bunkers which enabled him to survive those unbelievably heavy bombardments by General MacArthur's men in places like Iwo Jima and Okinawa, and later, in a different way, by both sides in the war in Vietnam, by which time the dugout and trench had degenerated into the foxhole, which was nonetheless a life-saving shelter or tactical position.

My main problem was with the caliber of the officers. Very few of those who had been given the rank had ever received any formal training as officers and fewer still understood the art of leadership and man management. Their main concern seemed more to do with the privileges and the pay that went with their appointment than with their responsibilities toward their men. As I explained to them on many occasions, an officer on his own is merely another soldier; without his men he is nothing. But an officer who is leading a group of men efficiently produces a unit in which the whole is greater than the sum of its parts. I spent some time teaching them how to care for their men, the point at which all leadership begins. And as it turned out they were able to witness an interesting case in point there and then.

One of my men, normally a cheerful sort of chap, began to lose heart and over a period of some weeks appeared to be suffering from some secret problem. I asked him if he would like to tell me about it, perhaps I could help. It turned out that he was married to a young girl in Salisbury, they had two children, and they had never been separated before. She hadn't written or answered his letters. That's all there was to it. OK, I said, no problem. We'll get the Red Cross to go round and see her and give us a report on how she's doing. He cheered up a little at the prospect. At his level he could see no solution to his problem. At mine it was simple. I got the Red Cross on the phone and set the thing in motion. Three days later they reported back—the young wife was happy but missing her husband, the kids were fine, everything was OK, not to worry. But why hadn't she written? Oh yes, she was sorry about that, but there was a good reason—you see, she had never been taught to read or write and had always kept that a secret from her husband. Now that he knew why she hadn't written he became himself once more. That

fact that she wasn't able to write didn't worry him in the least. For
my officers it was a good example in man management. The lesson
they had learned was that it is a leader's duty to use his authority
to care for his men, to do for them what they cannot do for themselves.

The caliber of the men in the unit was about the same as those I
had soldiered with during the war, except for one startling difference:
these men were all volunteers. A volunteer is worth ten pressed men,
as the saying is, possibly even ten conscripted men, and his attitude
to soldiering is consequently entirely different. One very seldom
hears a mercenary soldier moan, the besetting sin of most enlisted
men. He is there because he wants to be there, and he knows that
if he wants to break his contract he can do so. In these circumstances
he is enthusiastic to learn, to get fit, and to get into action. Because
of this a high standard of efficiency can be attained in a remarkably
short time. Furthermore, the knowledge that before long he will be
facing the enemy tends to concentrate his mind wonderfully. The
impetus this gives to training generates an exciting atmosphere and
develops a spirit of camaraderie, the very soul of soldiering, which
is vital to the success of small unit warfare.

These thoughts and experiences have led me to believe that a small,
well-paid volunteer professional army is preferable in many respects
to a large conscripted army in peace time. The latter disrupts the
economy of a country and serves only one vital requirement, that of
providing a reserve of trained or semitrained men who can be called
upon in an emergency to serve with the colors. Whether or not it
does that efficaciously is another question. The smaller fixed establishment also puts an end to empire building, the inevitable conse-
quence of ambitious unit and departmental commanders. But on the
other hand I would agree that a limited military training for all young
men, and women too, enriches the human quality of any nation. By
limited I mean three months of basic training followed by three
months in the field. This should be adequate for all purposes. Wiser
heads than mine also thought that six months training for a conscripted man in peace time was adequate, for was that not the period
laid down in March 1939 for Britain's first ever conscripted army?
They went by the old-fashioned name of militia.

But in some respects the years since the war had changed the
nature of the men. They were, in the main, more sophisticated. For
example, it was exceptional now to find a man who did not know

how to drive or maintain a motor vehicle. I remember serving in an armored unit during the war which had to begin its training by teaching 95 percent of its men how to drive. This inability to drive created serious problems in the training of mechanized units at the beginning of the war. By contrast Americans and South Africans, who came from countries that were highly mechanized—if I may use that expression to mean that they were familiar with motor vehicles and could drive and maintain them—were able to produce outstanding armored divisions during the war in an extremely short space of time.

But some of the sophistication of my men struck me as decidedly odd for soldiers on active service in the African bush. Perhaps that was merely because their average age was higher or that they had succumbed to the seductions of modern advertising. As part of my physical fitness training program and long after we had settled down to camp life and broken in our boots, I arranged a series of route marches on a progressive scale. These culminated in a thirty-five kilometer march from Jadotville to Shinkolobwe, a seven-hour grind in full battle order at a desired five kilometers in the hour, with a ten-minute halt every hour. Not exceptional for trained men, I hear you say, but not that easy either given the oppressive heat of the Congo.

At the third or fourth halt I made the men turn out their haversacks for inspection to check that they were carrying the prescribed items such as ground sheet, full water bottle, mess tin, eating irons, house-wife, washing kit, etc.—all the usual impedimenta without which an infantryman is presumed not to be able to fight. I was amazed to find that in addition to these things a large number of them were also carrying deodorants, after-shave, hair oil, shampoos, and the like. What the hell for? To smell lovely, I presumed. But for whom? I never discovered. I dismissed it as another of life's inexplicable mysteries. But thank heaven it was in the days before the Beatles had made long hair fashionable and thus there were no hair nets on parade.

I recall that when we were still about four kilometers from Shinko on that particular march one of my officers, an Israeli named Issy Bernstein who had joined the unit straight from Tel Aviv, asked permission to fall out and make his way to the Shinko post office independently. He was expecting an important telegram, he said, and had to get there before the place closed at 1700 hours. That gave him less than thirty minutes to cover the distance. I let him go but reminded him that he would have to run the whole way. Not something many men would want to do at the end of a gruelling day's march, carrying full battle order into the bargain. He went off like a jackrabbit and was waiting for us, telegram in hand, when we passed the post office an hour or so later. From this episode, and Lieutenant Bernstein's general behavior, I gained the impression that the Israeli army must be a tough lot of babies.

Why do men seek employment as mercenary soldiers? In general for the obvious reason that they wish to sell their skill as soldiers for money. They do not question the propriety of such an action, or its moral implications. The majority of them don't even know that such a question exists. They may be many things but very few of them are hypocrites. In the main I have found those mercenary soldiers whom I have commanded to be men in the real sense of the word, never small or niggling types, not any more cruel or licentious or bloodthirsty than their brothers in civvy street. Invariably they were generous and spent the money they earned with an easy abandon which of course made them attractive companions, the sort of chaps you would like to spend an evening out with. A small proportion of them were genuine adventurers, a breed that has almost vanished from the face of the earth, and these were not in the least bit interested in money. I often told my men that if they had volunteered for this way of life solely because of the money they would not last out the contract. It would occur to them sooner or later, particularly in the middle of the night when they were manning a foxhole, half drowned with rain and with the enemy taking pot shots at them, that there must be easier ways of earning a living. Very few of them seemed to worry about anything. The majority of them lived only for the day, and for that carefree attitude many of them were quite capable of citing biblical authority.

I tried to anticipate the tactics that might be needed in the Katanga in the variety of situations we might encounter. It was obvious that methods suitable for a European theater would be useless, if only because of the nature of the terrain and the unusual characteristics of the enemy. I began with a study of the enemy. He was unsophisticated, badly armed by our standards, but fanatically brave. Before any action he must fortify himself with marijuana and be under the influence of his tribal witch doctors. His tactics, in nearly every action, from the setting of an ambush to a frontal attack, amounted to the use of overwhelming numbers. These, I presumed, gave him courage and compensated for his lack of firepower.

Once more I sought the advice of the ex–Force Publique Belgian officers. They advised me that speed and noise were basic requirements when facing this type of enemy, and these tactics would succeed better than cautious approach by scouts, reconnaissance patrols, etc.—the tactics one might have used in Europe perhaps. Forget orthodox methods, they said, remember that great noise is associated with great power in the African mind and serves to intimidate the enemy.

In the same way firepower must be used to the maximum. Here it was not a question of counting your rounds and firing when you saw the whites of their eyes. That may have been right enough for soldiers who had carried their ammunition all the way from Cairo to Khartoum in Kitchener's time, but that was not the drill in the African bush. Here you saturated the possible target with fire whether or not you could see movement. It was enough merely to suspect it. Reconnaissance by fire they called it. This comforting advice ran counter to everything I had ever learned about the conservation of ammunition, but they were undoubtedly right. In these circumstances it meant that an almost unlimited supply of ammunition had to be built into the tactical plan.

Every man who was armed with an FN rifle or an M16 was now the equivalent of a light machine gunner, restricted only by the amount of ammunition he could carry or had immediate access to. With this firepower, four men with FN rifles were a potent force.

With these smaller groups, or subsections, I figured, must go a higher standard of junior leadership. Men with initiative, that much admired but little understood military attribute, would be needed more than ever. Thus ran my reasoning, and in the event I was not far off.

We were fortunate in having the use of a firing range close by. Exercises involving the use of live ammunition to teach fire and movement—"When I fire, you run"—were perhaps the nearest we could get to the real thing, although, regrettably, nothing can ever really prepare men for the trauma of actual combat. I suppose that's because the main ingredient, the element of fear, is missing. The

old army saying is absolutely true: action is like having a baby—
there is no adequate preparation for it. War films and television are
no help either. In fact they have a lot to answer for in creating false
impressions about combat. Movies, necessarily for their audiences,
have to concentrate on the hero image. Films give the impression
that wars are won by single-handed bravery in the face of impossible
odds. Real-life action teaches us the opposite: victory is invariably
the result of a team effort, the result of discipline, dogged determination, and patient obedience to orders, sometimes over a very
long period. Movies, largely because of the limitations of the film
frame, have to show men in close contact with one another whether
in defence or attack. In real-life combat the exact opposite is the
rule. Deployment and dispersion is the name of the game. Movies
make soldiers highly visible—necessarily so, otherwise there would
be nothing to see on the screen. Real-life action requires the soldier
to be as inconspicuous as possible. The average war film is not meant
to be a documentary. Is it any wonder inexperienced soldiers sometimes have entirely the wrong idea of warfare?

As I said, we were to be known as gendarmerie. While the name
evoked visions of red kepis, dark blue cloaks, and Place de la Con-
corde, it was not intended deliberately to mislead us. Very soon we
were told that there had been a change of plan and we were to be
used as an integral part of the army proper and not as a paramilitary
outfit in support of the army and the police, as the recruiting officer
had been told to tell us. In fact, when the implications of our intended
employment became more apparent several men decided to end their
contract then and there. Had the misnomers ended at that point it
would have been no great matter, but worse was to come, none of
it of our own making. We finally emerged in the public eye, and to
the world at large—which at that time was taking a great interest in
the advent of mercenary soldiers on the African scene—as part of a
group known collectively as *les affreux*, literally "the frightful ones."
I soon discovered, to my dismay, that this was a pretty accurate
description of those who had gone before.

The history of this little catastrophe was explained to me. About
four months prior to our arrival, the first Belgian mercenary soldiers
to join the Katangese Army had been organized in companies of
about one hundred men, in the proportion twenty Belgians to eighty
Katangese. These units were known as *groupes mobiles*. They were

mounted in jeeps and light armored vehicles and heavily armed with one MAG heavy machine gun, or .303 Browning MG, per vehicle. This highly mobile and very maneuverable strike force went into battle closely supported by Katangese truck-borne infantry with a devastating efficiency. Speed, noise, and immense firepower were their tactics.

They had certainly proved effective in putting down the Baluba rebellion in the north of Katanga. It could also be said that they had restored order, of a kind, to large parts of the country, which had witnessed all manner of atrocities at the hands of the enemy. On the other hand very many people in the Congo felt that this was a role better suited to the United Nations peacekeeping force, the very reason, one would have thought, for their presence in the Congo at all. Large numbers of these gentlemen were concentrated in Elizabethville and other parts of Katanga remote from the fighting, with apparently no great wish to embroil themselves in this unseemly quarrel. What they thought they were there for remained a mystery to many of us for months to come. The referee, it seemed to us, preferred to officiate from outside the ring. Later on in the history of Katanga, much to the amazement of the rest of the world, the U.N. peacekeeping chrysalis emerged as a full-fledged infantry brigade intent on nothing less than total war and destruction, which it waged mercilessly, assisted by Canberra bombers armed (but not piloted) by the United States and Britain, until Katanga was forced to abandon its independence and its president was sent into ignominious exile. However that is another story. And a sad one at that.

The Belgian and French mercenary soldiers of the *groupes mobiles* were without a doubt tough yeggs, and I do not criticize them on that score. Undeniably the situation in those parts of Katanga that had been overrun by Baluba had got completely out of hand and had to be dealt with swiftly and firmly. But it was their extravagant and unsoldierly behavior when back in Elizabethville and off duty that made me wince. Fresh from their conquests in the field they would swagger from bar to bar, crapulous, foul-mouthed, and quite unnecessarily armed. They dressed in what I came to call fancy dress—camouflaged jump jackets, indecently short shorts, shoes instead of boots, and socks rolled down to the ankle. Add to this picture of soldierly decorum a four-day stubble and you get the full unappetizing picture of an ill-disciplined lout intent on impressing the civilian population with his questionable toughness. In short, an unsoldierly mess. *Les affreux*, the frightful ones, were well named.

I wondered some about their reputed efficiency in battle, having rather old-fashioned notions about the relationship that I maintain exists between fighting capability on the one hand and soldierly turnout on the other. Surely to heaven the two go hand in hand? I never was able to satisfy myself on this point in the Katanga, but as far as the popularity of the frightful ones was concerned I was in a minority of one. The civilian population of Katanga had, in many cases, good reason to be grateful to these gentlemen, so I soon discovered to my chagrin that *les affreux* were in no way denigrated but, on the contrary, highly regarded and much entertained. Their unsoldierly appearance and swashbuckling behavior had been totally discounted. And the name stuck to all of us. Whether we liked it or not the title *les affreux*, as sponsored by the European civilians of Katanga and much publicized by the world press, was henceforth applied, without differentiation, to the entire *mercenariat*. It was something we had to learn to live with, like some congenital misfortune—a humped back or clubfoot, for instance.

But the press these types received was hard to live with. Every story was larger than life and in this the mercenary soldier had only himself to blame. If anything he played up to and encouraged the tough guy image. The odd part of all this is that in my experience it is usually the quiet mild type of man that is in there pitching when all others have fled, not the macho type described by one journalist some time later as "the sort of man you would expect to find walking down a road munching on a baby's arm."

This question of the relationship between a man's behavior in barracks and his subsequent performance in battle had always intrigued me. There was one body of opinion which held that the man who was forever in trouble and had a crime sheet as long as your arm in barracks was merely high-spirited and bored by training and army routine, and that when faced with the enemy and the challenge of action he would surprise us all and emerge a hero. I have to record that this desirable metamorphosis never occurred in any of the ruffians I have commanded. If they were a bloody nuisance in barracks they invariably turned out to be equally sanguine in action. In my opinion success in action is basically a result of sound training and disciplined behavior. Surely this must become even more essential when shot and shell are flying.

At the first full parade of my new command I made it abundantly clear that I wanted no frightful ones with me; every man would wash and shave every day without fail regardless of the difficulties or the circumstances, in action or out of it; a proper soldierly appearance and soldierly behavior were essentials if we were to succeed in behaving like a professional unit and imparting confidence to the civilian population who depended on us and to the people who paid us alike. I am happy to say that for the whole of this contract I never had reason to be ashamed of any of my men on this score.

The overall tactical position in Katanga at this time was fairly stable. The Baluba had crossed the Luvua River and withdrawn to the far north of the country, their traditional homeland. All the main towns throughout Katanga, north and south, were now garrisoned by the Katangese Army supported by *groupes mobiles*. Our role was, for the moment, to form the spearhead of a mobile reserve, which would be maintained at twenty-four-hour readiness. This brought me into closer contact with the Belgian staff officers at Etat Major in Elizabethville. I found them to be highly efficient and thoroughly professional, if a little insular, and more than somewhat jealous of their unique position in the Independent State of Katanga. Their military methods seemed to me, with my previous service—I had served for a time on General Auchinleck's staff at GHQ New Delhi during the war—to carry bureaucracy to absurd limits. Nothing seemed ever to be committed to paper in fewer than nineteen *exemplaires* and every possible document was given an elaborate number and typed to an exact formula. Army protocol was rampant. I never got used to it but you may be sure that Alistair Wicks and I found a suitable use for the inordinately large quantities of the gossamer bumf we received daily.

Just as our training program came to an end and boredom began to set in we got the call from Headquarters: report to Elizabethville at once.

Prepare for action.

3

The Nyunzu Column

"**C** 'EST *une belle colonne, n'est-ce pas?*" commented Commandant Grailly. He was the staff officer in charge of resupply, and in fact a sort of grand quartermaster to the Katangese Army. He had served many years with the old Force Publique and knew the Congo well. A most likable chap, painstaking and efficient. Now he was justifiably proud of his work. The column, which had taken him three long weeks to assemble, certainly looked beautiful—impressive anyway. My eye traveled down the line of new Ford five-ton trucks, each with a Katangese driver and two codrivers standing properly at ease by the front fender, awaiting inspection. There were fifty-one in all. Every truck was fully loaded and battened down with a camouflaged tarpaulin giving the column a romantic covered wagon look. If I'd had a stock whip I would have cracked it.

I followed the Commandant to Etat Major for a final briefing. 4 Commando was to escort the column to Nyunzu in northern Katanga, a major town on the railway line between Albertville on Lake Tanganyika and the terminus at Kabalo on the Lualaba River. The column was destined for the garrison at Nyunzu and contained urgently needed ammunition and rations, mostly evil smelling dried fish, manioc—the staple diet of the Katangese troops—U.S. Army C rations, and surprisingly, dozens of crates of Simba beer, without which, I was told, the Belgian Army personnel would find life insupportable. The total distance was 1350 kilometers and the route designated was due north from Elizabethville via Kilwa and Pweto on Lake Mweru, thence through Kapona and Albertville to Niemba and finally Nyunzu. This road was little used, explained Grailly, but as far as was known quite serviceable. He seemed a bit vague about this.

"Has anybody traveled over it recently?" I asked, with respect.

"Well, no, not for some months, but aerial reconnaissance tells us the surface is good for most of the way. I don't think you've got anything to worry about." Once more he didn't sound very reassuring.

We moved to the operations room to get the latest tactical position. A report had just come through that twenty Belgian priests had been massacred by the Baluba in a village near Kabalo and some sort of punitive action was being planned. We looked at a huge wall map of Katanga. An elegant staff officer explained with the aid of a long pointer:

"Once you have reached Pweto, there, and crossed the River Luvua, here, you will be in enemy territory, after which your chief danger will be from ambush. Speed therefore will be of the essence." And noise I was tempted to say, but resisted it. "The operation," he continued, "has been kept a close secret and it is considered unlikely that you will hit any trouble. The enemy will expect such a convoy to travel via the traditional main route which runs through Manono and Kiambi to Nyunzu. You will have therefore the inestimable advantage of surprise. Good luck. Any questions?" I had one.

"Yes. Is this the rainy season?"

"No. This is the beginning of the dry season. It extends from April to October. But I must warn you, it can be extremely cold at night."

I would like to have asked some questions about the state of the road but it was obvious they knew no more about it than we did and were simply hoping for the best. Strangely enough I had traveled this road a few years previously by motorcycle when I was doing what I thought was an adventurous journey from Cape Town to Cairo on a 350 cc AJS single cylinder machine. Part of this very road was described in those days by the Automobile Association as the "Trans Africa International Highway," a most imposing title for what I recalled with pain was the most diabolical track in Africa ever to be graced with the name of road, never mind highway. I also remembered that my trip was made during the so-called dry season, as now, and that I had sustained thirteen falls in one day on the slippery red mud that formed the surface of these roads in Katanga. But the gilded staff were unaware of my previous experience in the Congo and gave me the lofty treatment.

"Yes, well of course we see this as a fairly routine sort of job, don't you know. Shouldn't take you more than four days at the most to Nyunzu, always supposing you don't hit any trouble, that is. Three hundred and fifty kilometers a day—not excessive wouldn't you say? No need to hang about." I held my whist. Congolese roads had a sacred place in my memory. "In any case," he continued, "you will be in contact with us all the way by radio, and you can use clear. We have provided you with an LAD (Light Aid Detachment) and two or three qualified mechanics to look after any breakdowns you may have." From his tone of voice the mere idea of *dépannage* was unthinkable, if not positively disloyal. After all, the trucks were brand-new. What could possibly go wrong? What indeed.

Grailly walked back to the beautiful column with me, shook me by the hand rather too effusively I thought—well, warmly enough to put me on inquiry, was this perhaps the fond farewell?—wished me the best of luck and added, ominously, after making sure we were not being overheard, that in his view the main thing to watch out for was not the enemy but my Katangese drivers! These prophetic words zinged over my head to disappear into the wild blue yonder totally unheeded. Had I been killed on this trip they would have written on my tombstone: "He ignored a timely warning." But then, I was pretty new to the Congo.

I called an order group, gave out the route cards and the day's destination, emphasized that the road drill called for a vehicle density of ten vehicles to the kilometer, or dust distance, whatever that might prove to be, and that we should try to do fifty kilometers in the hour. This, need I say, turned out to be unbridled ambition. I would lead in my jeep with CSM Dowsey. 4 Commando vehicles would be interspersed throughout the column to lend confidence to the Katangese drivers who were even now a little bit jumpy and concerned for what lay ahead. There was no tactical consideration today, I said, it was only a question of movement. The radio truck would travel in rear of the column with the LAD and would maintain a listening watch the whole time. A young Belgian radio operator, a civilian, was attached to the column for this purpose. He wore soft pointed shoes and a nervous mien, neither of which inspired me with any confidence. Later we were to call him *grande vitesse* because of his incessant clamor for more speed. He was anxious to return home to his new wife, he explained, a worthy ambition which had my wholehearted sympathy, but one that rendered him worse than useless when the chips were down.

Stan Dowsey drove me in the leading jeep. We crawled slowly along the tarmac road to let the fifty-one trucks behind us unwind in an orderly manner and take up their proper stations. Ten minutes later I looked back at the formidable column traveling with the precision of an armored division. It was the one and only time I ever saw the column in anything remotely resembling order. A signpost said "Kilwa 364 km" after which the tarred road promptly expired giving place to a hard mud surface.

"Different County Council!" said Stan. He pronounced it "Carnty Carncil." His cockney humor was to be a tonic in the trial ahead. For the moment, however, all was well. A scorching sun baked us in our jeep despite the bush hats, and the prospect of two or three days like this before we were faced with more serious stuff in the shape of the Baluba, of whom we had heard some hair-raising tales, was not unpleasant.

I called a halt early in the afternoon so that the men could shake down to a routine, which I would introduce immediately. An hour before twilight I taught them the drill for Stand To, which they would now observe an hour before dawn and dusk, the most vulnerable times of the day in any defensive position. The long hour's tangible silence, accompanied by the incessant whirr of cicadas and a myriad insects, punctuated occasionally by the cry of the yellow hornbill as it swooped from low branch to low branch, dropped like a leaden cloak on the concentrated column and its two hundred silent and apprehensive men.

At Stand Down I sent Stan to inspect the column while Ted MacKay, who was now my batman and general factotum to our tiny mess, prepared the evening meal. On his return Stan reported that Auchterlonie wanted to see me. Apparently he was complaining that the men were ganging up on him. He reported that there had been a little bit of fighting among our men but nothing to worry about; it was more probable that Auchterlonie was a highly strung type and had been getting on the other men's nerves with his fanciful imagination. Auchterlonie was certainly showing signs of considerable agitation about something, which he could not define, but as he did not express himself in poetry on this occasion I thought no more about it. Nerves, I thought, and wrote it off as such.

We had reached Kapema, a village 160 kilometers from Elizabethville. Not a remarkable day's run all told but creditable in the circumstances. I went round the column during the night with one of the Katangese *sous-officiers* to talk to the Katangese drivers. The Belgian-trained noncommissioned officers were excellent soldiers. By contrast the vast majority of the Katangese drivers were raw recruits, civilians in uniform really, with perhaps two or three months basic training behind them, but enthusiastic about this way of life and cheerful enough at the moment. Most of them had only just been taught to drive, which of course made me more than a little apprehensive. I could sense some nervousness in them about the road ahead, but when I explained that our job was to protect the column and their's was to keep the trucks on the road they seemed less anxious. They took naturally to Sergeant Major Dowsey who had adopted the role of comedian for their special benefit. "*N'avez-vous pas peur; sergent-major est ici!*" shouted Stan in his execrable and cockney-flavored French, which freely translated was meant to be " 'ave no fear, Sergeant Major's 'ere!" At all events I do believe they took heart whenever they saw him.

I examined the loading and checked that none of the tarpaulins had been tampered with or the cargo broached. All was exactly as it was when we left Elizabethville. But the second and third days saw us in rougher terrain. The road had deteriorated and was now a mud track with a grass hump down the middle. From the greenness of the hump, and the height of the vegetation growing on it, I would say that nothing had been down this road in months. Deep ditches ran on both sides and separated the track from impenetrable secondary forest, which began about five yards away on either side. No light could penetrate that heavy foliage except perhaps at midday. It was quite obvious that no road maintenance whatsoever had taken place for several months. That was a serious matter. In this country the forces of nature were so virulent they would overrun a road such as this completely if left unchecked. Within a year it would be impossible to say it had ever existed.

After supper that evening I talked with some of the Katangese NCOs about the tribal history of their country. One of them who had been a schoolmaster was particularly knowledgeable and it was a pleasure to listen to him. Katanga had, it seemed, from time immemorial always been ruled by one of its two great tribes, the Baluba or the Lunda. The Baluba had formed a mighty empire several hundred years ago, which had stretched from Albertville on the shores of Lake Tanganyika westward across present-day northern Katanga as far as the province of Kasai, and as far south as 10 degrees latitude. In those days their empire was larger than Belgium and Holland combined. But like all empires it had waned and today the Baluba found themselves living as a minority tribe in northern Katanga, southern Kasai, and southern Kivu.

The rival tribe that took over from the Baluba was the Lunda, and this tribe under its great chief, Mwata Yama, had ruled over a kingdom greater in extent than Portugal. Their territory stretched from Angola in the west, through southern Kasai to southern Katanga, and south to include much of present-day Zambia. That was where we would find a lot of them today.

And there was yet a third and equally powerful tribe to contend with. This was the Bayeke, a fierce and warlike tribe, which had become a dominating force in Katanga in the middle of the nineteenth century under a ruthless chief named M'Siri. His capital had been at Bunkeya, a town that still existed not far north of present-day Jadotville. In those days Bunkeya was the greatest trading mart in Central Africa and had a population of more than twenty thousand people. M'Siri's cruelty had become a byword throughout the Congo, and his evil reputation persisted even to this day; people still living could remember how the palisades of Bunkeya were topped with the skulls of his vanquished enemies and those who had the temerity to disobey him.

These ancient tribal rivalries existed up to the present day. Mr. Moise Tshombe was a member of the Lunda royal house and had married the Paramount Chief's daughter. Mr. Jason Sendwe, the leader of the Balubakat, the political party of the Baluba in northern Katanga, had ties with the house of the royal family of the Baluba. And M'Siri's grandson, Godefroid Munongo, was the Minister of the Interior in the Independent State of Katanga.

The more recent history of the Congo was already well known to me; I prided myself on being what Mr. Tshombe once called me some years later—*un citoyen d'Afrique*. The Belgian Congo came into existence in 1908, and until 1956 politics and political parties were totally forbidden; the vast country was ruled by decree through a Governor General who took his orders from the Belgian government in Brussels. In 1956, however, the country took its first moves toward independence. These were in accordance with a plan originated by a Belgian academic named Van Bilsen. This plan envisaged the transfer of power to the Congolese in an orderly fashion over a period of some thirty years. The plan had an enthusiastic reception by the Congolese political parties of that time, which were then of course very much in their infancy.

The Van Bilsen plan might have been adopted had it not been for General Charles de Gaulle, President of France, who declared in 1958 that all French African possessions—and they were numerous and vast—could achieve independence immediately if they so wished, not in thirty years time, but now at once, *tout de suite*. In a speech made in Brazzaville, capital of the French Congo, the General repeated his offer. The fact that Brazzaville and Leopoldville are separated only by the mile-wide Congo River was of some significance. That speech and others made by General de Gaulle throughout the continent of Africa killed the Van Bilsen plan stone dead. Understandably the Congolese began to agitate for immediate independence too. This led to student unrest, demonstrations, rioting and bloodshed in the streets, and finally wholesale panic.

The feeling in Brussels was that the situation in the Belgian Congo could be normalized only by a promise of immediate independence for the colony. A Round Table conference was hurriedly convened in Brussels in January 1960 at which a Congolese politician, one Patrice Lumumba, emerged as the most potent force in Congolese politics. As he was also the only major Congolese politician to advocate a unitary system of government, as opposed to the federal systems suggested by Tshombe and some others, he found particular favor with the Belgians who saw the unitary government as a means of perpetuating their influence. The upshot of the conference was that King Baudouin of the Belgians confirmed a resolution that would grant independence to the Belgian Congo on June 30, 1960, in less than six months time!

Independence day celebrations in Leopoldville saw scenes of unparalleled jubilation marred by the erratic behavior of the new prime minister, Patrice Lumumba, who made a speech insulting the Belgian king and the Belgian colonialists in general. Four days later the Force

Publique, now known as the *Armée Nationale Congolaise*, mutinied against their Belgian officers and went on the rampage throughout the country, looting and raping. Their main grievance was that they, the army, had not benefited in any way from independence while on all sides their civilian brothers appeared to have done so. Lumumba redressed this situation by promoting every member of the army by one grade. This left the *Armée Nationale Congolaise* in the singular if unworkable position of having no private soldiers.

A week later on July 10, 1960, Mr. Tshombe, the president of the Conakat party and leader of the Katangese legislature, alarmed by the chaos that was sweeping over the Congo, declared Katanga to be an independent and sovereign state. The Balubakat, the minority party in the Katangese legislature led by Mr. Jason Sendwe, objected to this unilateral declaration and staged an armed revolt. Almost at once a ragtag army of Baluba warriors armed with shotguns, bows and arrows, and a few modern rifles crossed the Luvua River and seized the important mining town of Manono, which in normal times produced one-fortieth of the world's total production of high-grade tin. From this firm base they began to advance on the capital, Elizabethville.

A few days later Mr. Lumumba appealed to the United Nations to end Katanga's independence, by armed force if necessary. The U.N. immediately sent to the Congo the nucleus of a peacekeeping force, which was to grow in the course of the next four years into the equivalent of two light divisions, or 22,000 men.

Tshombe responded to the Baluba rebellion and the threat of United Nations action by raising his own army. This was to be trained and officered by Belgian officers on loan from the Belgian army, and supported at a later stage by several hundred Belgian and French mercenary soldiers. This new army, which was called *La Force Terrestriale Katangaise*, succeeded in putting down the major revolt by the Baluba and holding the ANC at bay. By April 1961 the main fire had been put out but several small ones still smouldered. Groups of lawless Baluba rebels were still roaming the country perpetrating atrocities, mostly against defenseless Belgian missionaries. It was the need to subdue this rebellious element of the Balubakat cartel and to defend the country against the possibility of attack by the ANC that formed the main reason for our employment in Katanga.

The fourth day we crawled along in the torrid heat smothered in thick layers of fine red dust, the vehicles in the rear stretching back over twelve kilometers. I prayed for the continuation of good weather and began to wonder what heavy rain might do to the track once fifty-one heavy vehicles had crossed it. I wasn't left to wonder for very long.

That evening we halted on the track and closed up head to tail for mutual protection, conscious that we were now on the edge of enemy territory. I kept the perimeter tight and posted a minimum number of sentries. There was only one possible approach to our position and that was along the track, from in front or behind. In any event an attack by night, the most difficult of military operations, was highly improbable by such an unsophisticated enemy. A possible danger would be accurate mortar fire, which, in our concentrated position, could be disastrous for us, but the 81 mm weapon was not known to exist in their armament as yet, so I discounted the risk.

Just after supper a commotion broke out in our lines and Alec Auchterlonie was marched in by Stan, disheveled and bleeding profusely from the nose. He had been fighting. Once more he accused his mates of having a go at him. This was absurd and would have to stop. I got the men concerned together informally and asked them to cut it out, if in fact it was true. I left it at that; it was not all that unusual. But Alec was convinced he was a marked man, no reason given. The next morning he asked if he could travel in the jeep with Stan and me. I agreed. Anything for a quiet life.

We were now about thirty-five kilometers from Kilwa, which was beginning to take on the attractions of a major metropolis. The weather was holding and the bright blue sky full of cumulo nimbus clouds which augured well. I was driving and Stan maintained contact on the PRC 9 with *grande vitesse* at the back of the column. Alec sat quietly in the back of the jeep. We were traveling at an average of thirty kilometers per hour. I then heard with some alarm that most ominous, distinctive, and unmistakable of all sounds—the ku-klux-klan of a rifle being cocked. I glanced round. It was Alec, fiddling with his FN. I hit the brakes.

"Take it away from him, Stan," I said.

"Nothing, Sergeant Major, nothing," said Alec, mildly, "just trying it out."

"Well put it down, lad. Don't touch it again, there's a good chap." Instinctively Stan, like all good managers of men, knew what tone of voice and manner to adopt in those circumstances.

Alec removed the magazine and unloaded the rifle. We moved off again. Stan had had some experience of people with mental illness and had told me the night before he thought Alec might be suffering from some sort of persecution complex. I felt it was unlikely. My guess was he was highly strung. Nothing more.

The road improved and the column gathered speed. Alec seemed more settled. But not for long. I heard a movement from the back of the jeep and looked around. Alec was standing up, clutching his rifle as he swayed from side to side, looking back down the length of the column. The next moment he stepped off the back of the jeep as naturally as though we were standing still. He hit the track, rolled over and over in a cloud of dust, got up, shook himself like a terrier, staggered to his rifle, seized it, and disappeared into the bush with the air of a man who was late for an appointment. A tough baby. A man could kill himself that way with ease. I jammed on the brakes and reversed sharply. Stan and I jumped out and followed Alec's track into the bush. Twenty meters into the forest we came to a dead halt. It was permanent twilight, as dark as dusk and almost impossible to move for thornbush, lianas, and undergrowth. It was impenetrable. We stood stock still and listened for any movement. Not a sound. Even the insects had suspended activity, disturbed by our invasion. All we could hear was the silence. The greenhouse atmosphere was all-pervading, oppressive, and damnably hot. We sweated.

"Alec! Alec! Alec!" called out Stan in a singsong voice that carried no distance. "Tea time! Tea time! Tea time! Grub's up, old son. Come on, lad, don't bugger us around. Nobody's going to hurt you." He pleaded. We edged further into the bush, Stan slightly ahead of me. I stood by the trunk of a large tree. "Play up! Play up! And play the game!" a voice called out from quite near by, followed by a low chuckle of glee, and then . . . crack and thump, simultaneously! A bullet hit the tree a foot or so above my head.

"To hell with that, Stan," I said. "I'm going to give him one more chance to come out, then I'm going to leave him."

"No, sir, you can't do that!" said Stan, alarmed. "Poor bastard will starve to death. What if the Baluba catch him?"

"Well, you tell him that. He's got his rifle, hasn't he?"

Stan tried again. Another shot rang out. Another maniacal laugh.

"You better go back, sir. We don't want you to cop it. I'll try on my own. Just give me a little longer."

I left Stan and made my way back to the track. It was absurd to risk being killed in this way. Stan took cover and edged his way forward from tree to tree calling out soothingly to Alec from time to time. Sergeant Major Dowsey was a patient and understanding soul and damned brave. But after half an hour he emerged from the jungle, torn and bleeding, and admitted he was beaten. I decided to wait for another hour to give Alec a chance to come out on his own. We brewed up tea on the track and waited. There was no sign of him. When the hour was up I organized a search party from my own men who went in line abreast, like beaters on the Yorkshire moors, calling out to Alec all the while. Still no joy. There was absolutely no trace of him. The forest had swallowed him up. Without a compass his chances of finding the track again were negligible. Even if he did I doubted if he would recognize it, that was what the bush did to you. It had happened to me twice in Bechuanaland years before when hunting—you stumble out of the bush on to the track and cross it without even recognizing it. Seems impossible, but it isn't.

It was a damned hard decision to make but I decided to leave Alec to his fate. Several of the men in his section, the ones who had been knocking him about in the last few days, didn't like my decision and told me so. They were certain I was sending Alec to his death. The psychology of soldiers is of never-ending interest to me and very often comes as a total surprise. It did so now. I could understand their point of view, of course, but it made no difference to me. They didn't have my problems. They weren't responsible for the column. I was.

I sent a signal to Etat Major and reported the incident, gave an exact map reference, and asked for a fighting patrol to be sent out at once to search for Alec. I could do no more. I blew my whistle and the column moved on.

4

The Melody Lingers On

Two days later we had almost reached Pweto, a garrison town and outpost at the top end of Lake Mweru. The lake is a massive sheet of water one hundred twenty kilometers long and fifty wide. It is fed at its southern end by the Luapula River, the first tributary of the Congo. At its northern end, where we now stood, the Luvua River flows out of it nearly a kilometer wide. It was the Rubicon for us. The other side was Baluba territory.

The Luvua then flows in a northwesterly direction for over two hundred miles before joining the mighty Lualaba, the next main tributary of the three-thousand-mile-long Congo River. In this manner the Luvua divides Katanga roughly into two parts, the northern part being the land of the six hundred thousand Baluba who migrated in times past from the adjacent Baluba kingdom of Kasai, the southern part being the land of the Lunda and the Bayeke.

The Baluba were a mighty nation whose number exceeded some two and a half million souls. They were brave, warlike, and industrious. Their villages were constructed with straight thoroughfares, which in central Africa was unusual because the straight line, unknown in nature, has no significance for the rural African. Furthermore their huts were square, not circular, another departure from the norm, for the African believes that the circle has no weak points, whereas the square has four.

Lake Mweru had been one of the objectives of Dr. David Livingstone's last expedition, which began in 1866 and ended with his death in 1873. The famous missionary had wondered whether the lake might prove to be the source of the Nile. Shortly before his death he had written to Henry Morton Stanley:

Eight days south of Katanga the natives declare the fountains of the
Nile to be. When I have found them I shall return by Katanga to the
underground houses of Rua . . . travel in boat up the river Lufira.

But Livingstone was destined never to find the fountains of the Nile.
What he had found without knowing it was one of the sources of
the Congo. When he got to Chitambo's village, some three hundred
miles south of Lake Mweru, sick and weary unto death, the great
missionary explorer entered in his diary for the last time
". . . knocked up quite." He died kneeling in prayer by his bedside.
In the morning his faithful servants, Susi and Chuma, those wonderfully loyal men, embalmed his body and carried it back safely to
Bagamoyo and then Zanzibar, a nine-month journey, much of it
through country harried by Arab slavers. He was buried a year later
in Westminster Abbey and the words on his tombstone are taken
from some he addressed to the *New York Herald* on the subject of
slavery: "May Heaven's rich blessing come down on everyone—
American, English, Turk—who will help heal this Open Sore of
the World."

The ferry could accommodate only two vehicles at a time so it
took more than a day to get the column across safely to the other
side. This gave the men a much needed rest and a chance to clean
themselves up and swim in the lake, disregarding its daunting reputation for bilharzia. This tropical disease is the work of a micro-
scopic parasitic snail that penetrates the skin and makes its way to
a man's liver with debilitating results, the most alarming of which
is that the patient begins to urinate blood. Not nice. Not nice at all.

Meanwhile I considered the choice of routes available to me from
here on. The shortest and most direct route was via Mwenge but
this was known to be strongly held by the enemy and a fierce action
would be inevitable. As Etat Major had decided against any trial of
strength on this occasion I confined myself to carrying out the main
intention, which was to get the convoy to its destination as safely
and as quickly as possible. The route via Baudouinville looked, therefore, as though it might be the safest if not the shortest or easiest
one to take. I began to think we might get to Nyunzu in about seven
days time.

It was only now that I was here, deep in the bush and in intimate
contact with the African, that I could appreciate the extraordinary

achievement of that famous explorer Henry Morton Stanley. Bula Matari was what his African bearers called him, the breaker of rocks. A hard man. Only an exceptionally hard man could have survived the three grueling years it had taken him to cross Africa from Bagamoyo on the east coast west to Kinshasa, the ancient capital of the Bas Congo, and beyond to the Atlantic coast, a distance of over three thousand marching miles. To say nothing of the steaming jungles and fast-flowing rivers that had cost him the lives of scores of his porters and the death of all three of his white officers.

That exploratory journey was the key that unlocked the Congo and its riches to commerce in the nineteenth century. It was financed and conceived by King Leopold II of the Belgians who used it as a catalyst to launch the International African Association, the forerunner of the Congo Free State. In the same year, 1876, Britain, Portugal, France, and Germany all agreed that the Congo Free State should have the status of an independent sovereign country and become the personal property of King Leopold. This amazing decision, the result of international intrigue, was confirmed in 1885 at the Berlin Conference. In an interesting footnote to history we find that the United States was the first nation to recognize the sovereignty of the International Association, preceding Belgium itself by a year. The Congo Free State finally became a colony, the Congo Belge, in 1908, when Leopold transferred all his personal rights to Belgium.

For the next fifty years the Belgians ruled the Congo directly from Brussels. Belgian industry and Belgian resources were used to develop the country's vast mineral potential, described by Jules Cornet, one of the early Belgian explorers, as a "geological scandal of riches." But in doing so the Belgians, unlike other colonial powers, did not encourage their nationals to settle or to own land in the colony. At the end of their contracts Belgian agents were normally obliged to return to Belgium. The towns and cities they constructed, in the face of immense difficulties, and the infrastructure of primary and secondary industry they created in the years in which they had supreme control remain as a lasting tribute to Belgian courage and fortitude. The administrative system they installed lives on to this day and is generally regarded as the finest in all Africa. I like to think that the Belgians were to the Congo (Zaire) what the ancient Romans were to Britain.

The night following the ferry crossing the heavens opened. We were now on minor mud roads, which became quagmires after the first four or five heavily laden trucks had churned up the surface. The trucks, which were the ordinary rear wheel drive commercial models, slithered off the track into the ditches or got bogged down up to their axles when the road collapsed under them. The rest of the column would then bunch right up. Sentries would be posted in the bush on either side of the track and the drill for underditching the vehicles would begin. This was a laborious and tedious process and meant completely off-loading the trucks, then cutting down nearby trees with which to build up the track. More often than not the final step was to jack up the chassis to let the wheels get a grip on something solid. The Katangese drivers were useless at this type of work, which called for patience, team spirit, and dogged determination. One by one we dragged the trucks back on to the road. It was time-consuming and backbreaking work, the incessant rain adding to our misery.

Underditching of vehicles is part of a soldier's training, and particularly so if he is a member of a mechanized unit. The drill usually presupposes that there is an anchor of some sort, perhaps another vehicle, stationed firmly on the road some distance from the ditched vehicle and that sufficient tow ropes are available to reach up to it. The anchor vehicle then drags the other one out or uses a winch. Where these facilities do not exist, as in our case, another useful method is to wind the vehicle out of the ditch by placing it in low gear and turning the starting handle against compression, with the ignition key off, of course. This works miraculously, the bogged down vehicle emerging inch by inch. But here again this method was not always available to us principally because the road itself had collapsed making the angle of the ditch impossibly steep. There was nothing for it but to build a new road under each vehicle. In circumstances like these we were most vulnerable to attack.

I called the officers and NCOs together and made general plans for our defense in the variety of situations that could arise. I stressed that even though the enemy were badly armed they were on no account to be underestimated. A Martini Henry shotgun manufactured in 1878 and charged with jagged bits of scrap iron could do more damage to you if fired at close quarters than a high-speed bullet, traveling at over three thousand feet per second, which passed straight through your body—always supposing you were that lucky. A seven-foot spear flung from a distance of thirty feet could transfix a man. The bow and poisoned arrow was not a child's toy. It was no laughing matter. At twenty to thirty meters a steel-tipped arrow would penetrate a man's chest to a depth of three inches and be impossible to withdraw, because of its barbs, without major surgery. And that would certainly prove fatal in our inexpert hands. If the arrowhead was poisoned with curare, which it was certain to be in this part of the world, a wounded man must lie as still as he could, the object being to slow down his pulse rate and blood circulation as much as possible. The last thing to give him was a stimulant such as alcohol or even tea. Even so, the result would nearly always be death within the hour.

I spoke to them about the old Baluba custom of ritual torture of their prisoners of war; the way adults of the tribe filed down their front teeth to a fine point; reminded them that cannibalism still existed in these parts and of the way in which the practice could be defended quite plausibly, to this day, by some of its advocates. Less than a hundred years ago the Baluba believed man was a carnivorous animal. Many of them probably still did for all I knew. Their reasoning developed along these lines. Was not human war merely man, the carnivorous animal, shedding blood like the lion and the leopard? The big animal seized the smaller one, the stronger man the weaker one. Did it not follow that you must eat what you killed? What animal killed wantonly just for the sake of killing? That was their general line of thought. Tradition died hard in innermost Africa, and not only among the primitive tribesmen. Quite recently the Leopoldville Supreme Court had found a Congolese ex–cabinet minister guilty of cannibalism.

I got the impression that most of my listeners didn't really believe these things happened in the twentieth century. But they do. The cultures of the Western world and primitive Central Africa are centuries apart. That is a fact of life. It is not, I told them, a question of which was better, or of mere comparison; that line of thought was pointless. Our judgment on that situation was superfluous and irrelevant. What we had to appreciate was that their culture was different from ours and that it existed. We had to deal with the here and now, not moralize about the differences.

Most of my officers and NCOs knew Africa only from their life in South Africa or Rhodesia, which I often pointed out to them was not Africa proper but something best described as Europe in Africa.

The real Africa begins north of the Zambezi, most of it deep in the bush far from the main road, and is seldom seen. Very few white men ever had the opportunity or the need or the desire to investigate this indubitable fact.

The morale of the Katangese drivers started to crack. They began deliberately to drive their vehicles off the road so that they could steal from their contents. Then they started to drink during the long hours in which they waited for their vehicles to be unditched. Their NCOs had absolutely no control over them. Those men who were fit for work, and there were very few of them, hadn't the strength to lift a fifty kilogram sack of rice. It was impossible for my unit to protect the column, unditch the vehicles, and discipline the hundred or so drivers who were stealing from the loads at the same time. I made an example of some of them with summary field punishments but it was useless. The rot had set in. They were not really soldiers but civilian drivers in uniform. The real Katangese soldier was a fine man, worthy of respect, tough, disciplined, and loyal, and I may say wonderfully humorous. These men for the most part were scum. I had no alternative but to let my own men take over their vehicles. This caused a near mutiny. Even though they were incapable of driving the trucks themselves they were unwilling to allow others to do so.

Progress was pitiful. In one day we notched up a mere fifteen kilometers, the whole day going in road making and unditching. The rain came down relentlessly, day and night, drenching every man to the skin. The track disintegrated completely and in places was no better than a stream of water. Now we could go neither forward nor back. I sent for *grande vitesse* to tell him to keep Etat Major informed of our plight. My runner returned from the back of the column to say he had found the radio truck empty. Our wireless operator had deserted at Pweto! He had, however, left a short note which explained that he was returning to Elizabethville because his radio had broken down and there were no spare parts for his set. This, he said, made it pointless for him to continue with us. Some logic in that, I thought, but a most unmilitary way of doing things. But perhaps he knew something we didn't. He was after all a *colon* who had lived all his life in the Katanga and probably knew more about the Congo and the Baluba than we would ever know. I ordered the sentries to be doubled at night, expecting an attack might be imminent.

These harsh conditions and real-life contact with men and the elements is what soldiering is really all about. The man who can raise a smile in these circumstances is a gem. Such a one was Ted MacKay. Whenever I felt like screaming at the Katangese or the weather or the road or the trucks ditched up to their axles in mud, there would be Ted with a steaming mug of tea and a joke. Nothing got him down. I think he must have been a direct descendant of that Tommy Atkins who stood in the trenches at Passchendaele in mud up to his putteed knees and went over the top to his death with unfaltering courage, following a boy second lieutenant whose expectancy of life in action was no more than sixteen days. God rest you, Ted, wherever you are.

We clawed our way northward, miserable kilometer by miserable kilometer. The route lay first toward Baudouinville and then Kapona, which I knew was fairly open country and therefore in all probability more favorable to us. I had in mind calling a two-day halt for maintenance and rest. Perhaps that would give the road a chance to dry out. If only we could have four hours of sun the track would be passable again. That I knew from experience is the general rule anywhere south of the equator. But the damned sun never showed.

The men were exhausted, demoralized, sodden with the continuous rain, and bloody minded. In many cases they looked as though they might be going down with malaria. Two bright sparks had contracted a spectacular species of gonorrhea, and it was four weeks since any mail had been distributed. All the makings of discontent were present. I discussed our situation with Stan and asked him how much more of this he thought the men could take.

"Got to give them a proper rest, sir. No good going on like this day after day. They're going to crack up pretty soon and then Gawd knows what will happen."

He was right. To press the men further would certainly have ended in disaster. I examined the map. Eight kilometers down the track was a Katangese Army outpost. Twenty-five kilometers beyond that was a small town. That dot meant there was an inn there. I figured that if we could make the outpost in another day I could persuade the Commandant de Place to guard the column for twenty-four hours while we, the escort, pressed on for the inn where we could have a rest and a cleanup. The prospect of a whole day's break would work wonders. If the men were told the plan they would perk up. From headquarters' point of view it would probably be viewed very differently, but I decided to risk it.

Two days later, about ten o'clock at night in blinding rain, my jeep slithered to a halt outside a double-storied building in a desolate village. Some faded red lettering on the wall above the bolted door proclaimed that this was the "Auberge de la Forêt." There was no sign of life.

"Do your stuff, Stan," I said. Stan hammered on the door with the butt end of his Browning pistol, the rain cascading down his ground sheet soaking his knees. There was no reply.

"Try again, Stan." The rest of the column closed right up, fender to fender, motors ticking over steadily as we waited, the jeep headlights throwing a milky glare into the vertical rainfall. The windows of the inn were shuttered, Mediterranean style, and everything looked bolted and barred. Damn it, just our flaming luck! I began to wonder if the place had been abandoned. It wouldn't have surprised me if it was. Suddenly a light flickered in a room on the first floor. That was better. Somebody was coming down the stairs. The heavy front door creaked open cautiously, and checked against a security chain. Stan spoke in muffled tones to a figure behind the door.

"OK, sir. *Bienvenue!*" Stan turned and laughed. He loved to think he could speak French. The men began to dismount and stretched themselves after the long ride.

I went inside to explain who we were and what we wanted. The Belgian patron, an ancient *colon*, thought nothing of opening the inn at this hour of the night to soldiers, but madame, tight-lipped in dressing gown and mobcap, hovered anxiously in the background wringing her hands in despair. She was *désolée*.

"*Pas de nourriture!*" she moaned.

"What's that all about, sir?" asked Stan.

"No grub, Sergeant Major."

I asked her if there was anything to drink and she said yes, there was, plenty. That suited us. We were long past hunger but a few beers would go down nicely. Could we doss down on the verandahs? Yes, of course, and they had some fresh straw in the stable. Lovely. But sorry again, there was nothing to eat.

"San fairy anne," said Stan (his father was in France during the Great War and had bequeathed him these anglicized pearls from the language of love, which he treasured). "Who wants to eat in the middle of the night anyway?"

"Belgians!" somebody said.

Simba beer there was by the crate, pastis, and whiskey galore. The men filled the bar, shedding their dripping ground sheets in the passage outside. When all the chairs were taken they sat on the floor with their backs against the walls, dampness oozing out of their clammy uniforms. Soon the place was jam-packed, lit by the warm glow of two or three paraffin lamps. The Belgian proprietors looked at us and each other with mounting dismay. They didn't like the look of the weapons for a start. Would we pay? And what might liquor do to us? Apprehension and alarm were written all over their faces. I put my arm round the patron's shoulders to reassure him. He was a good old chap. If they were kind enough to open the place for us, I told him, he had my assurance we would behave. I hoped I wouldn't have to eat my words; one never knew with some of these types. The old pair retreated behind the counter defensively and began to serve the men.

After the first few drinks had been downed a happy hubbub of conversation and laughter filled the room. This was more like it. The accumulated tensions and frustrations of the last fourteen days began to ebb slowly away, and finally to evaporate in that warm spirit of camaraderie known especially to soldiers who have faced common hardship and danger. It was, if you had stopped to think about it, a memorable moment.

Then it was time for a song. Stan got to his feet and rendered— his own expression—an old favorite loved by one and all, "Maybe It's Because I'm a Londoner." Stan had a ripe cockney tenor, trained, he once told me with pride and a hint of nostalgia, outside some of the best public houses in the Old Kent Road. Many the tanner he'd earned with a tearjerker when he was a nipper, he said, in his native Kennington. He began. The men quieted down. He put the heart-break in the right places and led the chorus, announcing the next line ahead of time in the best sing-along fashion. He got a big hand. Stan was a disciplinarian but had the maturity that came from much experience in the handling of men. A rare gift. At a time like this he knew how to take their back chat and ribald remarks without offense, pretty confident that when they were on parade again they would not take advantage.

"Song!" they all shouted, and an aspirant Mario Lanza obliged with deep breaths, much clearing of the throat, and eventually something from "The Student Prince." "Overhead the moon is shining," he began. But like the moon it was much too high. This earned him the bird amid some good-natured barracking. "Back to Sorrento, Mario," Stan advised, "safer that one, mate."

The patron was smiling now. He whispered to his wife. "Don't worry, *chérie*, everything's going to be alright, just like I said." But madame was still a little nervous. You never knew with *les anglais*, they had such extraordinary drinking habits. She hoped there were no *irlandais* among them. She shuddered. "You remember that time just after the war in Brussels, Maurice, yes you do, VE day . . . in the Place de la Ville, that man with the red hair . . . he was *irlandais*. . . . of course you remember . . . *nom de Dieu* how could anyone ever forget?" She shivered at the thought, and that had happened years ago.

We had been there more than an hour. The atmosphere was warm and cozy and smoke-laden. Suddenly the conversation ebbed into almost complete silence for no particular reason. Seamus Patrick Kelly shambled to his feet. He was an awkward sort of customer and nature hadn't been particularly kind to him in the looks department. He was a Liverpool Irishman from the Scotland Road. A failed civilian and an untidy mess as a soldier. For many good reasons he was the most unpopular man in the unit. The South Africans could not understand what he was saying half the time and the continentals did not trust him. He had taking ways, they said, the unforgivable sin in barracks. Kelly took a swig of beer and began to sing. Nobody paid any attention to him, just went on talking. Drinks were passed across him as he was singing—not deliberately, it was just that he didn't amount to much. But it didn't seem right to Stan. He called for a proper hearing, casting himself in the role of Chairman of the Palace of Varieties for the occasion.

"Fair do's, you blokes, give the singer a chance. Come on now, lads—ta ra! ra ra! ra ra!—I give you, Volunteer Kelly!" Most of the chatter died down. Kelly began again, stronger this time and with a little more confidence. Now we listened. I seemed to know that tune, sounded familiar, what was it, yes, hadn't heard that one in years. "Gentlemen Rankers Out on the Spree."* That was it. One

---

*Better known in the U.S. as "The Whiffenpoof Song."

of Bing Crosby's. Bit of Kipling, wasn't it? Kelly's voice was coarse but quite tuneful. You could tell he'd done a bit of singing in his time. No gimmicks, just straight from the heart. Gradually the talking stopped as Kelly's voice filled the smoky room. Then he swung into the chorus. One or two men with good voices picked up the refrain and began to harmonize with him.

> We're poor little lambs who've lost our way,
> Baa, baa, baa.
> We're little black sheep who've gone astray,
> Baa, baa, baa.

And then the rest of us joined in, good voices and bad voices, all together, swelling the chorus with an indefinable pathos.

> Gentlemen rankers out on the spree,
> Damned from here to eternity,
> God have mercy on such as we,
> Baa, baa, baa.

He sat down. There was no clapping and no laughter. Just an awkward silence. Kelly had put into words something nobody really wanted to hear. Soldiers of fortune. Loners. Many of us rootless. Far from home and loved ones—if any. God have mercy on such as we. Perhaps that was right, perhaps we were damned from here to eternity. One or two men stirred uneasily to hide their embarrassment. A barrage of swearing broke out, the subterfuge strong men resort to when they find themselves in an awkward situation. Somebody called for a round of drinks and the spell was broken.

Now Stan was waving to me from the other side of the room and pointing to his watch. It was one in the morning. I decided to let it go on for a bit longer. The therapy was worth ten dollars a minute. I left quietly, unobserved, as the mood clawed its way back to its former cheerfulness. Kelly and his song were forgotten, but something lingered on, damn him.

I lay on my bed and heard the songs again in the distance, bawdy and sentimental, cheerful and sad, coming and going on the wet night air. But at three in the morning all was quiet save for the pacing of the sentry outside my door, the crunch of gravel under his boots, and the comforting pitter-patter of rain on the iron roof above my head.

5

Katanga Mai

THE column resumed its painful progress, every kilometer northward bringing us deeper into the heart of enemy territory. I
stopped earlier than usual in the afternoon, closed the column right
up, and laid out the perimeter defenses myself. Here the bush was
not nearly as thick as it had been farther south and it would be
possible for an enemy to slink up to within a hundred meters of our
position undetected. In this case more of the Katangese drivers would
be needed to man the perimeter. That thought gave me pause. In a
position like this with untrained troops our main danger was more
likely to come from the reckless and uncontrolled fire of our own
men than from the enemy. I called the Katangese NCOs together
and impressed on them the need for the strictest fire control. This
was a nice time to start teaching the routine in the defensive position!

At twilight, during Stand To when all was quiet, we began to
hear the ominous beat of the tribal drums away in the distance. The
sound was aggressive, posing some sort of indefinable threat. A
warning, I supposed, but what were they saying, and to whom? I
asked the Katangese if they could read the message. They listened
hard. Yes, they said, they could. "The enemy are coming . . . the
warriors must gather." Now that it was pointed out to me I could
detect that there were in fact two distinct messages, two sets of
drumbeats, each being repeated again and again. If the interpreters
were right, we must expect an attack on the column pretty soon.

Just before midnight the sound of the drums grew louder and
louder. Now it was full of menace. I stood the column to again.
Most of the men were already awake and restive and took up their
positions willingly. Less than an hour later we began to hear the

sounds of wild singing and shouting coming nearer and nearer. This probably meant that the enemy were getting themselves hyped up for battle and massing in great numbers, their traditional tactics.

I could guess pretty accurately what would be happening on their side. A village not far from us would be their assembly area and here the witch doctors would dispense the *mai* to the warriors. *Mai* is the Swahili word for water. But in this case the witch doctors would cast a spell on it, turning it from plain water into a potent *muti*. The warriors must drink this as a medicine, while another small phial containing the *mai* would be given to each man to hang around his neck as a special protection. Then the warriors would be given *dagga* (marijuana) to smoke. They would kneel in a large circle while the witch doctors harangued them, stamping the earth and waving their short spears in their faces, encouraging them to fight, persuading them that now that they had taken the *mai* they had nothing to fear, they were invincible, the white man's bullets could do them no harm and would pass right through them. And in this they were, in the past, to some extent correct. Previously, whenever there had been any sort of uprising, the Force Publique or the police had been authorized to fire on the insurgents with blank cartridges and never with ball ammunition. The noise of the firing usually dispersed the mob. That way nobody ever got hurt, and out of this grew the belief that the white man's bullets would pass right through them.

So we waited for the attack, hoping to God it might never come. At two in the morning the noise of several hundred men moving steadily through the bush grew closer and closer. Now we could hear twigs snapping and branches being broken. The babble of voices grew to a crescendo. When I thought the enemy must be within a hundred meters of us I gave the order to fire five white illuminating flares in quick succession from Very light pistols. The brilliant lights burst from their tiny parachutes and drifted slowly to the ground, casting an eerie glow in the cold night air for over ninety seconds, bringing all activity to a sudden halt. Nothing moved. A moment later one of the men on the perimeter opened fire. Within three seconds every rifle was blazing away on automatic—at nothing! The noise was deafening. One minute later the main volleys ceased abruptly only to be followed by a few short bursts of desultory fire. Then those stopped. A strange silence blanketed everything. Gone was the shouting, the stamping of feet, the breaking of branches, the chanting of the warriors. Gone was the sound of the drums. All that remained was the acrid smell of cordite, which hung heavy in the air. The enemy melted back into the forest. The anticlimax was stupefying. We looked at each other in silence and wondered what was going to happen next. Nothing happened. We stood to for the rest of the night, on edge, and welcomed the dawn, which came in gray and wet. By the grace of God nobody had been killed by our own fire within the perimeter.

Part of the drill in every defensive position is the digging of latrines. Except in very unusual circumstances these are situated outside the perimeter and so can only be used by day. It is a strange comment on soldiers in the field that many of them are inordinately shy about using any form of crude latrine in public. Certainly those we constructed on this march could be described not only as public but primitive in the extreme. The construction is simplicity itself. A short trench is dug about one and a half meters deep and two meters long. A stout pole is suspended lengthwise over it so that it rests on two crossed poles at either end. The modus operandi follows naturally: drop pants, rest buttocks on pole, and aim judiciously. Not very dignified, of course, but that's how it often is in the field on active service.

I had warned my men on a number of occasions not to wander off into the bush on their own to do their morning devotions but to use the communal latrine. CSM Dowsey told them that during the war in Burma we had lost a number of good men this way, killed by Japanese snipers. But one man didn't listen.

Young Oakford was a modest sensitive type of man who had impressed me with his willingness to get stuck into every job that needed doing. He hated the embarrassment of the open latrine keenly. A small thing to most of us, but he loathed it. Just after stand down one morning in this particular position he went off alone into the surrounding bush. A sentry told me later he had heard a shout and then a single shot. He presumed it had been fired by Oakford, whom he had seen going through the perimeter. Puzzled he went to investigate, only to find the lad on the ground in the kneeling position with an arrow just below his ribs, paralyzed with shock. They brought him in on a mock-up stretcher to my headquarters. MacKay was also our medical orderly. He looked to me for instructions. I could suggest nothing. There was no question of trying to remove the barb, but Ted was able to break the shaft off low down without difficulty. Oakford was losing consciousness fast.

"I can dig it out if you think it wise, sir," said Ted, "but I reckon it's a bit too near his heart. Let me give him a shot of this." He held up a phial of morphine and a syringe.

"Do you know how to use it, Ted?" He nodded. At one time he had been a male nurse at Bulawayo Hospital.

But that was it, there was nothing else we could do. We stayed with him until he died, feeling helpless and miserable. His death shook us all and sent a shock wave of nervousness through the drivers in the column, reducing a number of them to near hysteria.

I am not going to torture you or myself with a description of the remainder of that nightmare journey. The rain continued in sheets, the majority of the Katangese drivers continued drunk and useless, and my men continued to do their work and our own until totally exhausted. Meanwhile the days dragged by. On the twenty-third day two men went down with malaria. We rigged up a sick bay in the back of a truck and covered them with blankets and gave them plenty to drink. There was little else we could do for them. The next day three more went down.

We were about a day away from Niemba. Alistair Wicks had received orders to patrol from Niemba to the Kivu border, so with luck he could be in Niemba with his half company. I knew he had a doctor with him, a medico named Donnelly from Springs in the Transvaal, and it was quite probable he had set up some sort of clinic there, perhaps even a small hospital. Meanwhile my men were going down thick and fast, throwing astronomically high temperatures one minute and shivering with cold the next—the traditional symptoms of malaria.

That evening a light plane flew down the road and dropped a bag containing official bumf, letters for the men, intelligence reports, and signals from HQ wanting to know what in the name of thunder did we think we were doing. Press on for Nyunzu with all speed, they said, your presence there is absolutely vital to the safety of the garrison, etc., etc.

One of the intelligence reports carried detailed information about recent actions against the Baluba in various parts of Katanga, with a few pages entitled "The Baluba Jeunesse" in a "know your enemy" style. I already knew that the Jeunesse, literally "the youth," formed the hard core of the rebel movement. The militant arm of political organizations throughout Africa is invariably recruited from these types, high-spirited and adventurous youngsters from about twelve to twenty-two years of age for whom the idea of warfare, the firing of weapons, and killing itself had a traditional appeal.

I read the intelligence pamphlet with professional zeal. If it was intended to fan hatred and loathing for the enemy, it succeeded. It went into horrifying detail of the atrocities perpetrated by the Jeunesse in this area in recent months and warned commanders of the consequences of allowing a man to be taken prisoner. Prisoners would be subjected to ritual torture, it stated. This was an unquestionable fact, and it must be appreciated that this was in the age-old tradition of Baluba warfare. A prisoner's fate would without any doubt be worse than death. The usual method was to tie the prisoner to a stake and begin by cutting off his arms above the elbow and legs below the knee. A sharpened bamboo stake would be forced up his anus while the witch doctor took out his heart while he was still alive. The object was to keep the man alive while the heart was still beating in the witch doctor's hands. Once dead he would be dismembered slowly and his flesh shared out to be eaten. Suicide before this dreadful end was preferable, the writer concluded. The writer was at pains to show that he was not exaggerating. He cited several well-documented cases. Two of them were:

A Belgian NCO named Leclerc was ambushed whilst on patrol and captured by the Jeunesse. His legs were cut off below the knees, his anus cut out, and his arms and legs skinned before his head was torn off.

The other was no less abominable:

Chief Vincent Yangala of the Manono District was captured in an ambush by the Baluba Jeunesse and condemned to death by a kangaroo court. His genitals were cut off, petrol poured over him and then set alight. His penis was carried triumphantly through the streets of Manono on a spearhead.

I passed this entertaining document around the unit for all to read, mark, learn, and inwardly digest. The information was not new to most of them but they were suitably impressed when they saw it set out in print. I began to think that in this part of Africa the primordial savage instincts that man was given in order to survive were still very much in evidence.

The following morning a scorching sun rose high in a cloudless sky and dried out that damnable road. Four hours later we began to roll again, slowly but surely, kilometer by kilometer into Niemba. I carried the Katanga flag* high on my jeep so that the outpost would know we were friends. At long last, there was the barrier. Was Captain Wicks here? He was. Thank God for that. The column rolled to a halt in the center of the village and we dismounted. We had taken twenty-five days to do a four-day march; one dead, one deserter, and twenty-two men down with malaria in 4 Commando; twenty-eight deserters and over forty cases of malaria among the Katangese drivers—to say nothing of the volume of goods stolen from the trucks. In short, a total disaster. Those Belgians were right; it was not the enemy that would kill you, it was the bloody country.

The village of Niemba comprised more than three hundred well-built and spacious huts, the majority in the usual Baluba square design, with thatched roofs and floors hardened with ant heap soil. Desirable residences. Several straight streets crisscrossed the village. In an open communal area the tribal talking drums were installed in their own special place of honor. Some wag had hung a label on the thatch shelter above them which said "Western Union." A whole row of huts had been leveled by the Katangese Army to make a landing strip for a light plane. One could believe from the look of the place that the Baluba were a highly industrious people, but at this time not one of the original inhabitants of this considerable village was to be seen. They had vanished deep into the bush, far from the main road, there to erect a duplicate village safe from the Katangese Army.

Captain Wicks had taken over the chief's hut as his unit headquarters. Alistair and I had become firm friends in the short time

---

*Red, green, and white with three red copper crosses on the white. The green was for the jungle, the red for the blood spilled defending their independence, and the white for the purity of their women, so Mr. Tshombe told me some time later.

we had known each other, and I was delighted and relieved to see him once again. He was calm, well-bred, intellectual, and astute. He had been educated at Harrow and Oxford and spoke excellent French and some German. This in itself was bordering on the unusual in a man who had been brought up at a time when Englishmen setting foot on the continent were advised to speak slowly and clearly in English and to raise their voices as necessary to make the foreigners understand. His manner was always gentle, and his sense of humor light. In all the years I was to know him I never knew him sour or critical of anyone. But now he took some delight in ribbing me softly. "What happened, old chap? Took the wrong turning somewhere I suppose? The map, the map, old chum, you really must learn to read the map. You had us worried, you know. Mustn't dawdle like that. Here, drink this, dear boy, and you'll feel a lot better."

He was right, nothing like three fingers of Scotch to ease the burden of leading two hundred assorted villains on these accursed roads. I stood the column down and handed the sick over to Dr. Donnelly. His little hospital was functioning well already.

After a delicious bath in a canvas tub, with Ted pouring jugs of hot water over me as we sang "Down by the Old Millstream"—Ted torturing it on the mouth organ—and other vocal gems from our repertoire, life began to return to normal. In that moment of physical well-being I felt supremely happy, as though life had nothing better to offer. Which at that precise moment it hadn't. Contrast is the name of the game, my son.

"Feel like a little social visit this evening?" asked Alistair.

"No," I said, emphatically, "I feel like three weeks in bed if you really want to know. Why?"

"I've been invited to call on the Commandant de Place, name of Palmois. Must be a Belgian with a name like that. These Belgiques usually have a good table. Come along if you feel like it. I shall be leaving about five."

Alistair Wicks always behaved as though he were living at his regimental depot in the heart of England. He was a hangover from the gracious days of the Empire when men of his station in life dressed for dinner regardless of the difficulties. At five his driver reported for duty. Wicks was resplendent in a kilt—his family was from Scotland—which Sandy King had made for him, a jeweled *skein dhu* much in evidence below one knee.

"Coming?"

I dragged myself off the string charpoy and tottered out into the evening air.

Wicks believed in arriving in style. Less than four hundred yards away we stopped in front of a modest thatched hut. We were welcomed by a grubby individual who introduced himself as Lieutenant Palmois (not his real name) but pronounced it Palmer, English fashion, which was absolutely right and proper, for Lieutenant Bertie Palmer was as English as a bowler hat. We saluted and then shook hands. The Palmois bit was to suit the Belgians, he said; they had problems with his name, which usually ended up as Palmaire. He led us into a bare room where we sat on soapboxes around a low wooden table.

Palmer was not, need I say, Commandant de Place or Commandant of anything else for that matter. Closer acquaintance with Bertie revealed that he was a genuine fake and as rough as a warthog's arse to boot. He was in command, he claimed, with a dramatic look over his shoulder and a lowering of his voice, of a small group of Katangese scouts on a special mission from the Minister of the Interior, Mr. Godefroid Munongo, but he was unable to tell us what the mission was, old chap, wish I could don't you know but can't, all in one breath which, incidentally, stank. Official secret. He tapped the side of an ample nose with a fat forefinger. His shirt and trousers were filthy and bloodstained and he sported a four-day beard which contrasted sharply with his shaven dome. He wore two revolvers and a bandolier of assorted ammunition. Bare feet completed the fetching ensemble.

He was, I imagined, living up to his own idea of the full-blooded *mercenaire*. There was nothing humble about him. Nothing much military either. I sincerely doubt from my subsequent knowledge of him whether he had ever had a single day's formal military training in his life; but at this moment nobody knew that and he was able to play the role of the tough military specialist to the hilt. And he played it very convincingly. Like quite a number of mercenary soldiers I met in the Katanga and was to meet later in the Congo, he was able to get away with this make-believe reputation through sheer bravado. The pretense might have fooled 90 percent of his audience all of the time, but not Alistair or me. We had had more cold dinners than he had days service in the army, we figured, and laughed him off.

Bertie had been at the grog for some hours prior to our arrival, I would say. Now he was entering the garrulous stage. He slopped us out two whacking dollops of army issue rum, which we drank out of dark green C ration tins with twisted wire handles. The tins were marked "Frankfurter and Beans." We listened politely to his flow of baloney. He wanted to impress us. Cuba was his last assignment. Really? And Korea? Of course Korea. Izzatso? Ya, the Yellow Wall—man, he'd like to tell us about that frightful episode, but please, excuse him, even now it brought on nightmares. It went on and on, all genuine no-carat stuff. Alistair goaded him on wickedly. The Legion? He began to sing the Legionnaire's song in atrocious French but broke off abruptly. Memories, he said, becoming maudlin, and muttered something about Sidi Bel Abbes and the pals he would never see again. Alistair offered him a spotless white handkerchief. He ignored it. He plugged straight on. He had an unlikely story for every theater of war since VJ day. Then he belched, farted broadly, and lurched out of the room for a minute.

"Colourful character," I said to Alistair, yawning hugely behind my hand. "Might have made a happy little buccaneer in Elizabethan times. Bit of an anachronism really."

"Anachronism my arse," muttered Alistair, with rare acidity. He was never able to share my enthusiasm for nature's small-part character actors. "Nothing but a two-bit bullshitter!"

We wrote him off in our minds and prepared to accept him in his own amusing role. If it had ended there we could have forgotten all about Bertie and gone home to bed. But it didn't. Bertie returned, his fly undone. He sloshed out three more drinks.

"Any Baluba around here?" asked Alistair sociably, knowing he was inviting a torrent of unlikely anecdotes.

"Plenty. The bastards are everywhere. Just off the road . . . in the bush . . . waiting, always waiting. You can't see the sods but they're there alright. Watch out at ant hills, they love those. If they cop you with an arrow you've had it. Eleven minutes to die, *mon capitaine.*" He bared his arm at the shoulder. A large patch of raw skin about the size of a cap badge looked as though it had recently healed.

"Arrow!" he said, simply.

"Did you live?" asked Alistair. Bertie ignored the shaft.

"Lay doggo, old chum. Had my faithful Askari feed me whisky until the effects wore off!"

We laughed at the nonsense. Wicks was still laughing when we heard a noise like a body hitting the floor in the room next door. The noise *was* a body hitting the floor in the room next door. I raised an enquiring eyebrow.

"Oh him!" said Bertie. "Want to see a Baluba prisoner? Askari! Come here, you miserable bastard."

A smart black soldier wearing a red fez, an ex-Askari from the King's African Rifles, came in. He saluted smartly and then murmured *jambo bwana* and bowed briefly to each of us. I spoke a few words to him in Swahili. The Askari avoided my eyes. He was probably a deserter.

"Bring that bleeder here!" shouted Bertie.

The Askari sprang to attention, executed a smart about turn, and marched off short. He wanted to show us he was the real McCoy. He led in a pitiful object which clanked to a halt in front of us, a stocky Maluba* clad in animal skins and heavy leg irons. Manacles were clamped on his wrists and attached to the leg irons by a heavy chain. One step away from death but still with a faint glimmer of pride and defiance in his bearing. God above, I thought to myself, the human spirit is unconquerable. From his nose to his chin where his mouth should have been was a bloody mess. One arm hung limply at his side, unnaturally, probably broken. Festering sores covered his bare legs. A swarm of hungry greenbacked flies feasted on them. The stench of him was overpowering. With all that, there was still something inexplicably noble in the way he held his head up.

"Clout him!" ordered Bertie.

The Askari struck the Maluba on the side of the head with a short baton, completely without emotion. Thwack! The Maluba staggered a pace or two and collapsed against the wall. His eyes glazed over and he focused on infinity.

---

*The prefix Ba before the name of an African tribe means "the people of." The prefix Ma denotes a person of that tribe. Thus Baluba, the people of the Luba tribe, and Maluba, a person of that tribe.

"Wake him up a bit, Askari!" shouted Bertie. The black soldier unsheathed a commando type dagger whose blade was razor sharp. With the point he drew a vertical line down the Maluba's stomach from his navel as far as his pubic hair. Globules of blood followed the point as he pressed the blade down and in. Alistair and I looked at each other. This was bloody ridiculous. I got angry.

"What's this in aid of?" I demanded.

"Persuasion!" said Bertie, spinning the cylinder of a .38 Smith and Wesson over and over again, nonchalantly, blowing down the chambers, Humphrey Bogart fashion. "Knows where the other bastards are hiding in the bush. We've got a score to settle with them. Killed two of my Katangese boys last week. I'm going to make this sod talk if it's the last thing I do. I've given him until dawn to tell us what he knows. After that . . ." He put the revolver to his head and pulled an imaginary trigger.

The nonsense had gone far enough.

"Don't be bloody absurd, Palmer," I said. "This is inhuman. You're not a sadist are you? There are proper ways of handling prisoners; you know that. Send him back to Commandant Jacques at Albertville for interrogation in the proper manner."

Palmer rose, furious. He had been showing off and now his act was being taken apart. He exploded with anger.

"Proper manner! Christ Almighty!" he screamed. "Where the hell do you think you are? This isn't the 8th bloody Army at Benghazi. Geneva convention and all that crap! This is the Congo, man. This is darkest bloody Africa! You don't know the Baluba, do you Captain? They're not soldiers. They're savages, bleeding savages. Do you know what will happen to you if they capture you—which heaven forbid, *mon capitaine?* Do you want me to tell you? They'll tie you to a stake in the centre of the village, then they'll cut your hands and your feet off. Then they'll stick a bamboo pole up your arse. Then they'll start to take your skin off—you're still alive—and then they'll take your heart out while it's still beating. They can do it too, I'll tell you, they've had plenty of practice at it. Ritual torture! Ever heard of it? And you call me inhuman! Christ, man, you don't know the meaning of the word."

"We are civilized, or supposed to be, Palmer. We know they're savages. We apply our standards, not theirs. That's the difference."

He rounded on me viciously, knocking over his rum.

"Captain, do me a favor will you? You run your bloody war the way you want to, just leave me to run mine."

He had gone too far. But there were no Queens Regulations here. No Army Act. It was the strength of one personality against another, nothing more. But I was the senior officer.

"Lieutenant Palmer, you listen to me and listen good! And Captain Wicks, you witness what I am going to tell him. Tomorrow morning at first light you send that prisoner back to Commandant Jacques. That's an order! If I hear he hasn't got to Albertville I shall have you arrested and tried for murder. You hear me?"

We stood eyeball to eyeball. Like all bullies, he backed down. We left. I had a vague disturbed feeling I might be wrong. This was the bush after all, and what did I know about the enemy? Nothing really from first-hand experience. Could Palmer be right? This was not war as I knew it. This was the Congo. Palmer probably knew more about it than I did. Wicks backed me up, as always.

"Don't be absurd, Mike. Of course you're right. Palmer's a bloody head case, but I can't see him killing the prisoner, not after you warned him of the consequences."

Alistair saw us off the next day just before dawn. The road from Niemba to Nyunzu was forty-five kilometers and ran through some very heavy sand belts and thick bush. Once more progress was pitifully slow. About twenty-five kilometers out of Niemba the column bogged down, this time in the sand. We were in up to the axles again. Our last tow rope had snapped. Night fell.

In the morning I sent my driver, Frank Hastie, back to Niemba with an armed escort to borrow more tow ropes. At noon he was back.

"The Maluba prisoner?" I asked him.

"Shot at dawn," said Frank.

"Did you see the body yourself?"

"Yes, sir."

6

Breakout from Nyunzu

NYUNZU was described on the maps as a Chief Place. Its normal population was greater than that of Niemba and its huts spread over a wider area, but in a less orderly fashion. A sandy street ran straight through the middle of the town for about half a kilometer, keeping parallel with the railway line, which ran east-west some three hundred meters to the north. On either side of the street a few straggling coconut trees struggled to survive. Some boarded-up shops and a few brick bungalows in a derelict condition told their story—the Baluba inhabitants had long since departed. There was no trade, no market, and no civilians. The town was at a standstill.

At the far end of the road was a crossroad. A building on one corner, with a much-cracked stucco facade, boasted a sign which said "Territoire," indicating that this was the headquarters of the local administration. The Katangese flag hung listlessly from a flag-pole on the first floor. Immediately opposite, behind rows of barbed wire, was the headquarters of the Commandant de Place, Commandant Liegeois. About three hundred yards farther down the main street was a tented compound for a battalion of the Malay Regiment, part of the U.N. peacekeeping force. Apart from the Katangese military presence, Nyunzu was a ghost town.

My HQ and mess were a hundred meters or so from the crossroad, and my men were billeted in houses just off the main street about two hundred meters from Area Headquarters. I reported my arrival to the Commandant and arranged for the column to be handed over formally. Liegeois, who was a Belgian regular army officer on sec-ondment to the Katangese Army, was a short, stocky individual never to be seen without a cigarette in his mouth. He was a member of the Chasseurs Alpins and wore the floppy green beret that distinguishes that famous regiment from other units in the Belgian Army. He had a reputation for firmness and efficiency. He received me somewhat coolly, making it plain he thought I had been dawdling on the way up from Elizabethville; however, he was a fair man and gave my subsequent report a decent hearing and said he was only too aware of the problems such a journey entailed. He was, I knew, a very experienced officer with many years service in the old Force Publique. Despite our poor start I grew to respect the little Commandant as a man of great professional integrity and personal courage.

At this moment he was busy getting Nyunzu going again. His aim was to encourage the civilian population to leave the bush and to resume normal life under the protection of the Katangese armed forces. I presumed that they were reluctant to accept this somewhat dubious invitation because of the heavy-handed methods of *les affreux* in the area some weeks previously. But before the population could return the town had to be made reasonably habitable. The supplies of water and electricity were nonexistent to begin with, and these were the two problems Liegeois was giving top priority at this moment. The diesel generator that produced the electricity was broken. Parts for it were to be flown in by light plane that afternoon, and he had given instructions for a landing strip to be specially prepared about eight kilometers east of the town, just north of the road to Niemba. The water supply came from a concrete reservoir about a kilometer due south of the crossroad, deep in the bush. The enemy had destroyed much of the pump house and machinery. This would have to be repaired. Could I send out a patrol and get the motor going? I said I thought I could as, fortunately, I had a diesel mechanic in my unit. To reach the reservoir we would have to take a fighting patrol and cut our way with pangas. After that I was to erect a strong, barbed wire barricade around the whole installation and arrange for it to be patrolled once daily as part of my unit's duties.

I reported the state of my unit, which was now less than 50 percent effective owing to the large number of men down with malaria. Captain Donnelly, the medical officer, was still supervising their treatment. That evening he reported that he expected more men would go down with the disease in the course of the next few days. Recovery might take an average of ten days, after which the men would require a period of convalescence, perhaps as long as two weeks.

Those who were fit for duty would be required for patrols along the railway line from Albertville to Kabalo, which it was vital to keep in operation. Apart from that no major operations were planned, the Katangese Army presence being entirely administrative. We were to maintain a low profile. Liegeois took pains to explain that the enemy was the rebellious Balubakat Jeunesse, the ones who were perpetrating atrocities, not the entire Baluba nation. It was the ordinary tribesmen we must try to entice back into their villages to resume a normal life.

I handed in my report on the journey, which ended with a full account of the episode at Niemba with Lieutenant Palmer and the Maluba prisoner. I repeated my request that Palmer should be arrested at once and brought to trial. Liegeois passed no comment at the time but later in the day he sent two Belgian officers with an escort to arrest Palmer and take him to Elizabethville for summary court-martial. For the moment I forgot the affair. Other matters were demanding attention.

To find ourselves cheek by jowl with the United Nations forces in the same small town was a little disconcerting but not without precedent. The *casques bleus*, blue helmets, as they were called, among other things less polite, were by no means certain as to how they were required to carry out their peacekeeping role in Katanga. In particular there was a considerable doubt in their minds as to the degree of force they were authorized to use to maintain law and order should that become necessary. Furthermore, they would have welcomed a firm directive from the Security Council as to the precise circumstances in which such force could be used.

The ambiguity of their position stemmed from a Security Council resolution dated February 21, 1961. It stated, inter alia:

> Deeply concerned at the grave repercussions of these crimes (the killing of Patrice Lumumba, Maurice Mpolo, and Joseph Okito) and the danger of widespread civil war and bloodshed in the Congo and the threat to international peace and security . . . and noting the development of a serious civil war situation and preparations therefor:
> The Security Council:

1. Urges that the U.N. takes immediately all appropriate measures to prevent the occurrence of civil war in the Congo . . . the halting of all military operations, the prevention of clashes, and the use of force, if necessary, in the last resort;
2. Urges that measures be taken for the immediate withdrawal and evacuation from the Congo of all Belgian and other foreign military and paramilitary personnel and political advisers not under the U.N. command, and mercenaries.

It was generally considered that the resolution was vague and uncertain, particularly paragraph 2. In no manner did it lay upon the local U.N. commanders a clear-cut and unambiguous duty to expel *all* non-Congolese military personnel; it merely urged them to take measures to do so. Furthermore these local U.N. commanders must have wondered, as we did, whether the Security Council really meant they were required to expel *all* Belgian military personnel, when it must have been quite obvious to them, as it was to neutral observers, that the Belgian military presence was the mainstay of the Katangese Army, and without that presence chaos would come again.

As a result of this uncertainty it was only to be expected that local U.N. commanders would interpret their mandate in widely different manners. For example, in Manono, where the Baluba had previously overrun the Katangese garrison, the U.N. peacekeeping unit had stood stolidly by and taken no action when the Katangese forces, aided by the White Legion, counterattacked and recaptured the town. But in Kabalo some weeks later the local U.N. commander of Ethiopian forces had taken it upon himself to arrest the White Legion, which comprised thirty or so mercenary troops, just as they were about to disembark from their aircraft. Plainly he needed very little urging. His interpretation of the resolution completely ignored the Belgian military presence on this occasion, but empowered him to arrest and expel mercenaries. Later the same commander of peacekeeping forces saw fit to bombard and sink with mortar fire a river steamer that was ferrying Katangese troops, Belgian officers, and civilians to Kabalo, with enormous loss of life. On no interpretation could this barbarous act have been authorized by the U.N. resolution.

Things would turn, it seemed to me, very largely on the temperament and character of the local U.N. commander. Everything must depend on how he saw his duty and how he intended to interpret the famous resolution. In situations such as Nyunzu, the personality of the U.N. commander would be of the first importance. Who, I asked Liegeois, is the local U.N. commander? What sort of a chap is he?

As it turned out we were very fortunate. The local commander was one Prince Nazirmuddhin, the officer commanding the Malayan Regiment, apparently a very able and well-respected regular army officer. The Belgians spoke highly of him. Certainly his unit was well disciplined and displayed all the hallmarks of military efficiency: good turnout, high standard of saluting, excellent vehicle maintenance, and so on. It was thought improbable that the Prince would make any unexpected attack on any of us or try to arrest us, Belgians and mercenaries alike, with a view to expulsion under the terms of the resolution. It was more likely he would use a diplomatic approach in the first instance, some sort of ultimatum perhaps. Even in warfare of this sort chivalry had its place. In the event I was not far off in my estimate of this fine man.

In these circumstances the proximity of the U.N. troops was a cause for some concern to us. No way were we any match for one thousand well-armed U.N. soldiers equipped with Ferret armored cars and three-inch mortars if it came to a showdown. I examined the alternative courses of action available to the Malayans. The most probable and logical one was that they would try to arrest us, peaceably in the first instance, but with force in the second. I began to make a plan. All ranks were informed that in the event of an action of this sort the unit would disperse into the bush on a prearranged signal and make their way to a place known to all of us, namely the concrete reservoir. If this happened the men were to come prepared for a four-day march through the bush. Once we had gathered at the RV we would make the detailed plan as required. Everybody understood this. Each man's immediate action was to prepare his kit for such an emergency so that it could be snatched up at a moment's notice.

After a few days some of my men began to recover from malaria, but those who were seriously ill were evacuated to Albertville by a four-seater Cessna civilian aircraft which visited us from time to time. The plane was piloted by an indestructible little Canadian named Max Glasspole whose devil-may-care attitude was probably better suited to the Royal Flying Corps of 1915 than Katanga 1961.

Three previous planes piloted by the intrepid Max had bitten the Katanga dust, but he had walked away smiling from each one of them. Max's routine was to buzz the town on his arrival so that a jeep could go out and collect him at the airstrip. As he invariably brought mail and hard liquor there was always a rush to greet him, and very soon he achieved a popularity second only to Father Christmas.

On this occasion he brought with him a passenger, a young officer of about twenty-one who had been posted to my unit. Second Lieutenant Simon Donaldson was tall, black-haired, and exceedingly handsome. I took an instant liking to this personable young man who radiated confidence and ability. He behaved as though he had had some formal military training but I doubted that he had been an officer in the Horse Guards, as was rumored prior to his arrival. Even so he was a natural leader of men and I could see he would quickly gain their respect despite his youth. Rumors circulated about some of his more daring escapades against the Baluba while attached to a *groupe mobile* before he had been laid low with a bout of malaria, the illness from which he had just recovered. One of these stories told how he had dispersed a mob of two thousand Baluba without firing a shot. He was a born adventurer and had the makings of a first-class officer.

Simon had an interesting background. He had been educated in England and spent some part of his youth in Tanganyika where his father, reputedly immensely wealthy, had some interest in a diamond mine. His grandfather was the famous Colonel Donaldson, a founder member of one of the great Johannesburg mining houses and known throughout South Africa for an educational foundation he had set up to care for black miners. Simon knew Tanganyika well and spoke Swahili like a native. We found common ground in our love of ocean sailing and he told me of the time when he had crewed in a thirty-six-foot ketch that had run into difficulties off the French Atlantic coast in very bad weather, as a result of which they had to abandon ship. The French Navy eventually rescued them after a ten-day search financed by his father. He made a living in various occupations, a recent one being as a model for a prestigious fashion house in London. He ran an apartment in Mayfair and was part of the London social scene, which bored him to tears. He was a great admirer of Mr. Tshombe and believed in what he stood for in Africa.

When he read that the president of Katanga needed officers for his armed forces he wrote to him offering his services and received an immediate reply. So here he was. For my part I was extremely glad to have him. Officer material of this caliber is a rarity in any army, and especially so in a mercenary unit. I gave him his own command at once. If he had a noticeable fault it was only that he had a tendency to act on impulse. This did not worry me at all as in certain circumstances, for example in action, it could be a distinct advantage.

The medical officer's daily report indicated the seriousness of our position. Twenty men were awaiting evacuation to the hospital for various illnesses. The journey up, the bush, and the unrelenting climate had wreaked havoc with their health. CSM Dowsey and I were among the few still unscathed. It is very probable that he and I were left untouched by the anopheles mosquito simply because we did not stand guard at night for such long hours as the men. In addition I always slept under a net, come what may. Stan's theory was that we both drank whiskey. I think there must be something in this as I have noticed that men who drink whiskey are often immune from malaria. It's a good excuse anyway, if one needs one. I am not a boozer but on campaign, or whenever I am on safari, I always travel with a case of Scotch whiskey in my baggage. Ballantine's for preference—I find the rectangular bottles convenient for stowage. Come sundown a glass or two helps relax the muscles, eases nervous tension, and repels the cold night air. Taken in moderation, of course. On the other hand I have found on many occasions, especially at sea in a yacht, that the belief that alcohol will warm you up is a snare and a delusion, even though it seems to have that momentary effect. What it does in fact is to give you a temporary glow which wears off quite rapidly in cold weather and leaves you worse off than when you started. This is due, I am told, to the fact that alcohol expands the surface area of the skin's blood vessels, which then cool off more rapidly when they come in contact with cold air.

One Saturday morning about eight o'clock Simon accompanied the Sergeant Major and me on an inspection of the lines. As usual the Sergeant Major preceded me into the billets with a shout of "Stand up! C.O.'s inspection!" In one hut we found three of my men, all Swedes, sitting around a bamboo table drinking beer with a very attractive young black girl. Dowsey had an apoplectic fit. I mention it only to illustrate how far from regular soldiering mercenary soldiering can be, and why the need for discipline is even greater in the latter. I noticed as we were walking that Simon had a slight limp and asked him about it. Yes, he said, he had picked that up in a small accident, showing some Belgian officers how to drop off the back of a jeep at thirty-five miles per hour. He was over it now, he said, but confessed a long march would probably knock him up a bit. As long marches on these roads or through the bush were the last thing I had in mind I never gave it another thought.

On arrival at the mess the doctor said Ted MacKay was going down with malaria but was refusing to be evacuated to hospital. Ted was now our majordomo at the mess and had taken a great liking to Simon, whom he looked after like a favorite nephew. Simon reciprocated the friendship. He thought he could nurse Ted through his illness if it got any worse. They made an odd pair, Simon being six foot four inches tall and Ted five feet two. I let Ted stay.

Late in the evening of May 6 I received an Immediate from HQ Albertville. It was a warning. They had intercepted a U.N. signal ordering the Malayans in Nyunzu to arrest 4 Commando at once and send the unit to Leopoldville as prisoners. No action was indicated by HQ; it was only what it said, a warning. I hurried down to our lines and stood the unit to. We surrounded the billets with Dannert wire and erected sandbagged firing points at strategic places. I wanted to give the impression we would resist if any attempt was made to take us by force, while at the same time knowing full well resistance was futile. During the night my patrols reported that the Malayans, whose compound was barely six hundred yards away, were unusually active, as though making preparations to move out.

At dawn they began to warm up their Ferret scout cars.

But nothing happened. An hour after dawn I assumed the danger to have passed and stood the men down. It must have been a false alarm. I returned to my headquarters with my officers. We were all greatly relieved that it had not come to a showdown with the United Nations unit. The thought of opening fire on the Malayans was repugnant to the majority of us. Many of us had fought side by side with them in Malaya only a few years back and had a great admiration and respect for the well-disciplined brown men, some of the finest soldiers in the world. We regarded them as old friends.

It was eight o'clock in the morning and we were drinking coffee in the compound outside our mess. Suddenly two Ferret armored cars and two truck loads of Malayan infantry drove rapidly into our courtyard and took up threatening positions, training their weapons on us. We continued to drink our coffee, bemused. A Malayan major approached me, saluted politely, and informed me I must consider myself under arrest as of this moment and would I please accompany him to their HQ. Their colonel wanted a word with me. I indicated to the major that I would be obliged if the theatricals could be abandoned. He ordered his men to lower their rifles. I went quietly. As I went I whispered an order to Simon to place the men on alert and to be ready to put our emergency plan into operation.

His Royal Highness Colonel Prince Nazirmuddhin was an officer in the finest Sandhurst tradition from the shine on his chin strap to the brilliant polish of his brogues. He explained in a reasonable tone that his orders were to take my unit prisoner and that he was anxious to do this without any bloodshed. I countered, in the same tone, that my men were hardened mercenary soldiers (heaven help me!) with very little to lose, and that I did not think they could be taken prisoner without a fight, which I would be loath to have with old friends. Our conversation was carried on in this highly civilized manner. I was hoping the colonel would regard me as an honorable opponent not to be confused in any way with *les affreux*. He went on to explain that the U.N. Security Council resolution of February 21 empowered the United Nations forces in the Congo to disarm, arrest, and expel all mercenary soldiers from the country. I said that the U.N. resolution was largely unknown to my men, which was the truth, and that if he gave me the opportunity to explain it to them some of them might feel disposed to surrender. Perhaps we could begin on that basis? The Prince was of two minds about this request but finally decided he would allow it.

"You give me your word as an officer and a gentleman you will return after you have spoken to your men?" he asked.

I made no answer. If he should ever read this story written after all these years I would like him to know I felt bad about that, but my hand was forced. I also had my duty to do and that duty very clearly was to avoid capture at all costs.

I walked down the road to the men's billets. They were already assembled and in a state of readiness to move out. I outlined the position we were in, read the U.N. resolution of February 21, explained what it might mean, and then said there were only two courses of action open to us: one was to surrender to the Malayans, which would mean being sent to Leopoldville as prisoners of war, like the White Legion before us; and the other was to escape into the bush and make our way to Niemba, our nearest base, and that this would entail a considerable risk. For one thing it would mean a march through the bush of over fifty kilometers, which might take as long as four days and, to put it mildly, would be one hell of a trip. Not to mention the possibility of bumping into the Baluba Jeunesse.

A discussion followed at the end of which the majority said they would prefer to take their chances in the bush than submit to surrender. One South African became positively emotional when he recalled his imprisonment by the Germans after Tobruk. No surrender for him, he said, never again, never, never, never. Seven men said they were prepared to surrender.

I made a plan and issued orders for the escape. Prepare for a four-day march. Battle order to be worn. Carry as much food as you can, fill water bottles full, and when I blow my whistle you dash across the road into the bush and disperse in every direction and then make your way individually to the RV point, the concrete reservoir, as swiftly as possible. The seven men who were to surrender must go up the road first and kick up as much dust as they could so as to attract the attention of the two Ferret armored cars which were covering the road. When they were about fifty yards from them they were to start a fight between themselves. Under cover of this diversion we would make our dash. The Ferrets might open fire on us as we crossed the road but I doubted it. Any questions? Yes, sir. It was Simon.

"I've got a jeep hidden in the bush by the side of the landing strip. I left it there yesterday. I don't think I can make the march with my leg in the condition it's in. Nor can Ted. He's damned sick. Will you let us make our way to the jeep on our own? Once we get away we can meet you at the 15 km stone later on. What do you think?"

It was a good plan and it could have worked, but unfortunately the Malayans were already on the strip with their Ferrets.

"No, Simon. On your own you stand no chance. Fall in with the others. You too, Ted." It was the last order I was ever to issue to those two brave men.

I sent the seven men up the road. I waited until they were halfway along it and nearing the Ferrets and had started their little fight before I blew my whistle. From all sides my men dashed across the road into the bush. Not a shot was fired. We scrambled through the undergrowth and an hour later arrived at the RV from all directions. Stan called the roll hurriedly. The doctor had been caught as he was leaving the mess. There was no sign of Simon Donaldson or of Ted MacKay. Nobody had seen them. The Malayans must have got them too. Everybody else had got here safely.

I gave orders for the march. We would try to get back on the Niemba road about ten kilometers from Nyunzu. This would mean two jinks through the bush, the first about five kilometers southeast, the second at a right angle to it about eight kilometers northeast. We could expect to make a little less than one kilometer in the hour. There was no track to follow, we would have to slash our way through virgin bush. We would go in single file, well spaced out. Des Willans would be the pathfinder and leading scout. He would have to take his direction from my compass. I would count the steps.

The sun was already high in the heavens and the day promised to be blisteringly hot. We set off without any further delay, glad to be on the move again but wondering how near the Baluba Jeunesse might be. Des Willans was a superb soldier. He was about nineteen, a fine physical specimen, and until recently a regular soldier in the Rhodesian Light Infantry where he had been selected for training as a cadet officer. He had joined Tshombe's army about six months previously with a genuine desire to help the Belgians in those early days of chaos. He had never received any pay for his services due to some administrative foul up, nor did he expect any. He was quite happy to soldier on. He was the oddest mercenary soldier I ever met. Now he was the only man in the unit fit and strong enough to hack a path for us to safety. He began to slash at the bush with a panga, methodically, step by step, untiring, unruffled, and unafraid. The column advanced into the head-high undergrowth to be swallowed up as though it had never existed.

After about fifteen minutes a chopper thwacked its way into view and hovered above us at about three hundred feet. Fortunately the column had just entered a belt of trees. We froze and lay stock still, faces down, hands under bodies. Nothing white showed and nobody made the slightest movement. The temptation to look up was over-powering. I covered my face with a camouflage scarf and focussed my binoculars on the cockpit. There was no door. I recognized the pilot, a Canadian attached to the U.N. forces. I had had a drink with him in a bar in Elizabethville quite recently. A good guy. We could have shot him down with no trouble at all, but it would have been pointless. He must have been able to see where we had entered the forest too, our track would have glistened in the sunlight and been quite visible from the air, but after a minute or so he banked sharply and scooted off. Subsequently I heard he reported no trace of us. It was a strange sort of war. Perhaps he thought we were good guys too.

At the first halt I realized that very few men were fit enough for a junket of this sort and I was beginning to wonder if they would be able to make it. But it was too late to turn back now. The four-week convoy had knocked the stuffing out of most of them and they had not had time to recover. Some men began to discard bits of their equipment, something I had always regarded as an unforgivable sin but had to overlook now. It was going to be a question of survival. The enemy was the terrain, rules and regulations would have to be ignored.

Willans was still in the lead slashing away steadily. From time to time I could see his head bobbing up out of the bush. It was un-mistakable. He had given himself a Mohican haircut, his head completely bald but for a ridge of hair down the middle of his bare scalp. He claimed he was the only man in the unit with a built-in coon cap. I continued to count the steps and now I reckoned we were barely making half a kilometer in the hour. It was eleven in the morning and the sun beat down fiercely. Where the hell was the rain when we wanted it? With luck, if we did not get lost, or hit the Jeunesse, we might make the road by nightfall, which in these parts was at 1830 hours.

For short periods I had Des relieved as lead scout and changed the rear guard every fifteen minutes. The job of rear scout was exhausting and vital to our safety, for it was from behind that our greatest danger lay. I had not forgotten that a ten-man patrol from an Irish battalion of the U.N. forces had been attacked in these very parts by the Baluba Jeunesse last November, less than six months ago. Nine of the patrol were massacred, one escaped. The Baluba

Jeunesse found the sole survivor later in the bush and beat him to death. It was known that the patrol had been overtaken from the rear.

We halted every hour. Then every half hour. Suddenly for no reason the bush cleared and we were able to make a few kilometers unhindered before striking the dense bush again. At the halts the men began to eat their rations and drink their water as though there was going to be a fresh issue at the end of the day. Many of them were totally inexperienced. It was too late to try to teach march discipline, but a few of the old sweats conserved both these vital elements just in case. Des, who was now carrying two rifles, brought me a piece of wild sugar cane which gave me instant energy—and an almighty thirst. What I really wanted was to find a banana tree, which would have meant both food and water, but we were not that lucky. Not just yet anyway.

I called a long halt. The men were exhausted and plagued with insect bites. Some were beginning to get down-hearted. I heard one say he thought I had got them lost. Another one said, "Don't be a bloody fool. He was in Burma. This is nothing new to him!" In fact it was nothing like Burma but exactly the same as parts of Bechuanaland where I had spent much time hunting and on safari in the Okavango delta. In any case it was a cast-iron certainty that we would reach the road if only we persevered. Look at the facts. I had been able to see the sun all day, I knew the road ran due east-west, and I had a compass and a map. What more did I need? It was a simple mathematical proposition. We were going to march on two sides of a right-angled triangle. The Nyunzu-Niemba road was the hypotenuse. We must hit it in time. Perhaps not exactly at the spot I was aiming for, but that was unimportant. But what was worrying me, and was much more vital, was the possibility that we might not reach the road before nightfall. Once we were on the road we would have a clear field of fire if we had to defend ourselves against the Jeunesse. An action in the bush would be another matter.

I decided to let the men rest while Des and I went on ahead to reconnoiter the way to the road. By my reckoning it had to be less than one kilometer away. After an hour of comparatively swift travel, unencumbered by the slow pace of the column, we broke through the bush and saw it. What a sight! Less than one hundred meters away we saw a brick-built causeway carrying the road! And under it a series of culverts through which a beautiful clear stream was trickling fast, the sunlight dancing on it even now. Unbelievably, one bank of the stream was lined with wild banana trees! Come to Daddy! The grass was higher than either of us as we gazed on this enchanting scene, spellbound, thinking only of getting to the water as quickly as we could. But a moment later we froze. The steady drone of motor vehicles broke the silence.

Three Ferret armored cars with their turrets open stopped in the middle of the causeway and closed up. The Malayans were patrolling the road looking for us. The crews got out. I counted them, six in all. That was right, two to each car. They chatted to each other and looked over the side into the stream. One or two began to pee into it. Some smoked cigarettes. Des raised his FN and drew a bead on one of them, a sergeant, probably the leader. The range was less than a hundred meters. He looked at me inquiringly. I pushed his rifle down by the muzzle and shook my head. Negative. Des mimed "Why not?" The armored cars were empty, the men would scatter, maybe we would have to kill or wound one or two of them, but we would end up with three vehicles. It was the logical military action. But I did not alter my decision. Perhaps I was wrong but I have never regretted it. Apart from other considerations there is something repulsive about firing at an unarmed man. After a few minutes they mounted and drove off again in the direction of Nyunzu. I concluded from that, wrongly as it turned out, that this was as far as they were patrolling.

I sent Des back to bring the column up, no mean feat in bushcraft, and gave him my oil-bath prismatic compass and the back bearing. As soon as Des had gone I made my way to the bridge, got under the end culvert, stripped off naked, and had me a bath. Ten minutes later, to my considerable alarm, I heard the noise of motor vehicles approaching. This time from the east. I dashed to my clothes but I was too late. There was no time to dress. I sank below the water, my head just above it. Three Ferret armored cars coming from the Niemba side stopped on the causeway immediately above me. The crews dismounted and after a moment or two began to pee into the water. So did I! Five minutes later they threw cigarette ends into the stream and moved on. I breathed again.

An hour passed and Des brought up the column. The first and most difficult part of the march was over. I posted sentries with whistles a good way down the road on either side of the bridge while the rest of the men enjoyed a bath and a drink, which restored their spirits. Then they gathered bananas and had a feed. Night fell, its jet black cloak wrapping us in a feeling of security. We marched tactically in the dark for another ten kilometers straight down the road to Niemba, in total silence, weary and worn, and then took a track off the main road to a deserted village for the night. Tempting though it was I decided we would not sleep in the huts, despite the cold, but in the open bush close by. It would be safer that way. The night air was perishingly cold so we huddled close to each other for mutual warmth, arms entwined, two by two, Frank Hastie being my intimate companion for the night. Just as I was dropping off to sleep he murmured in my ear.

"Can I ask you something, sir?"

"Yes, Jock. What is it?"

"Do you still love me?"

I shudder to think what a sensitive Baluba scout stumbling on our prostrate forms would have made of our strange behavior that night.

Two days later, footsore and ravenously hungry, we made our weary way into Niemba. A man led me to the chief's hut. Captain Wicks was playing bridge with his officers.

"Don't tell me you got lost again," he quipped. "Every time I see you these days you need a bath."

But he was optimistic about Simon and Ted. "Must be in the bag. Don't worry about them. Wait, I'll get Liegeois on the blower. He's sure to know."

But after talking to the Commandant on the radio and reporting our arrival in Niemba we learned that the Malayans had not captured Simon or Ted. He confirmed that Doctor Donnelly had been caught and sent to Leopoldville already. The other two must have escaped at the same time as us. But where were they? Had they made their way to the jeep by the landing strip after all? I hoped not. Two men in a jeep on their own in this part of the world could be in great danger. I was sure they appreciated that.

We rested. A few days later Commandant Liegeois sent my unit transport through to Niemba and we were mobile again. In the meanwhile I had signaled all local headquarters informing them that two of my men were missing, with details, and asking them urgently for any information they might have. I gave the number of the missing Jeep, which was 236, painted in black on a white background, front and back. I waited hour by hour for news of the two men but none came. I began to fear some terrible disaster might have occurred. This was the Congo. Anything could have happened.

The attitude of the U.N. Commander in northern Katanga was now made clear. He issued an order to arrest all mercenary troops in his area while leaving the Belgians in the Katangese forces alone to run the show. As a result Etat Major ordered my unit to return to base, Shinkolobwe, as quickly as possible. There was to be a new role for us. A large camp had been set up in Elizabethville to accommodate Baluba refugees and this would need guarding.

The immediate return to Shinko was the most popular order I have ever issued. As in life, so with soldiering: everything is relative. During the war my regiment was posted to Poona on its arrival in India from the U.K. In our newness and our ignorance of the country we hated it. A year later after knocking about all over Bombay province, mostly under canvas, we came to regard Poona for what it was, the pearl of all Indian semi-hill stations. So it was with Shinko, which now would seem like paradise after this God-forsaken bush littered with burnt-out villages, rain-sodden tracks, and a brooding unseen enemy.

7

The Fighting Patrol

W E returned to Shinkolobwe in less than four days, traveling via Manono. In our absence many-high level decisions had been taken in the political arena which were to affect our future employment as a mercenary unit within the *Force Terrestriale Katangaise*, and to lead eventually to our disbandment. But for the moment we were not aware of them.

We were met on arrival at Shinkolobwe by a singular character who informed us that he was now our new commanding officer. He was a Frenchman, Major Roger Falques, late of the French Army, or possibly on secondment from it, I never knew for certain. His career in the Katanga prior to this was fairly well known and he had the reputation of being a ruthless and bold commander. I paraded my unit. He inspected my men swiftly with the efficiency born of much actual contact with soldiers, and stood us at ease appreciating that the men had just returned from the field and were tired. He ended by asking me if I hadn't any wounded—*vous n'avez pas de blessés?*—in a tone which suggested that to return from an operation without any wounded was some sort of disgrace, at best an indication that we had not tried very hard. Fortunately I had one man on crutches whose leg was suitably encased in plaster, which gave the right impression. I didn't tell the Major he had fallen off a truck, the result of a bit of horseplay.

He invited me to his villa for a drink that evening. We drank Scotch whiskey, neat. *"Pas de l'eau!"* he regretted, adding in his rather limited English, "Water . . . no good . . . *radioactif!*" which was probably true in this place. We discussed the military and the political situation at considerable length. The latter was highly volatile at this moment. He then gave me the first of two far-reaching items of news. Mr. Tshombe had been taken prisoner by the Central Government while attending a conference of Congolese leaders called to consider the ending of Katanga's independence! Even now, he went on, Mr. Tshombe was languishing, inexplicably, under house arrest in Coquilhatville, the capital of the Equatorial province of the Congo, which of course must be regarded as enemy territory.

This treacherous piece of behavior on the part of President Kasavubu, Falques continued, was certainly not in keeping with the spirit of reconciliation that had animated Mr. Tshombe when he agreed to meet with his compatriots. That, I supposed, explained the poster I had seen in Jadotville on our way through to Shinko just a few hours before. It showed a sad portrait of President Moise Tshombe, and under it the poignant words, *"Il souffre pour nous. Soyez digne de lui."* He suffers for us. Be worthy of him. To what extent, if any, the population reacted to this noble sentiment I never discovered. But for us, admirers and followers of the President, it was an event of considerable importance and one fraught with a latent danger.

The current political situation is a matter for the constant consideration of any mercenary commander in the field. If he values his skin he must keep abreast of it at all costs. He could wake up one morning and find that the government or politicians who employed him are out of office, leaving him and his unit in an invidious position. Not to mention the consequences of a nonexistent paymaster—a chilling thought. But in normal circumstances he should be immune from internal political problems and perfectly safe if he adheres to the terms of his contract with his employers, who should be, preferably, a democratically elected government—a consummation devoutly to be wished but one very seldom encountered in the Africa of today.

The other earthshaking item of news was that the Katangese government had decided to phase out the majority of the Belgian officers in the Katangese forces and to replace them with French regular army officers on secondment. What do you think of that! The major examined me closely for my reaction to this blockbuster. I am sorry to say I must have disappointed him. In default of anything more expressive all I could think of on the spur of the moment was, *"Sapristi!"* I might also have added *"Tiens!"* and shown him the palms of my hands, but I don't remember.

To be truthful the politics of Katanga and the Congo were completely beyond my ken at this time, try though I did to keep abreast of their rapid changes. Frankly I could not see that the substitution of Belgian officers by French would make the slightest difference to us in 4 Commando, and as it turned out I was quite right. The French also did everything in nineteen copies, but of course with considerably more panache.

Major Roger Falques was a man who commanded instant respect. He was tall, wiry, and tough. There was not an ounce of superfluous fat on the man anywhere, I would have guessed. His face was pock-marked and weather-beaten, his hair close-cropped. A saber scar ran vividly down one cheek, conjuring up visions of duels fought in Saigon, Ventiane, or Phnom Penh. Part of his right thumb was missing and a wound elsewhere had removed the curvature from one buttock. Altogether he had suffered twenty-two wounds in as many years service under the French flag. He was the sole survivor of his year at St. Cyr.

He had served with the French Army in almost continuous action since he was first commissioned in the year the war broke out, and in recent times he had fought in French Indochina and been evacuated from Dien Bien Phu at the eleventh hour of that grueling operation. He had also been an officer in the French Foreign Legion and quite recently he had been staff officer to a division in Algeria. His substantive rank was full colonel but because of the unusual rank structure of the Katangese Army he was now a major—he shrugged his shoulders. Yes, I said, the circumstances had affected me in much the same way. I added with understanding and in English, I find myself in the same boat. Same boat? The colloquialism floored him. Major Roger Falques was a professional soldier through and through and it would be an honor to serve under him. I said as much and meant it.

But in a day or two I began to feel the sweep of his new broom. My unit was now back as a full company, with Alistair Wicks as my second in command. Major Falques sent for me. He had been studying my establishment and seemed perturbed.

"Vous êtes trop riche!" he exclaimed, vehemently. I was intrigued. Being rich, never mind too rich, has always been one of my cherished ambitions, but regrettably not one I have ever been able to attain. Why I was too rich followed immediately.

"You have eight officers for only one hundred fifteen men!" He
said it as though I was willfully cheating the Katangese government
in some heinous manner. This criminal state of affairs was to cease
forthwith.

"Do you know that in the Legion we have only one officer, one
sous-officier and one *adjudant-chef* to one hundred men?" he added, by
way of comparison.

I said I was comforted to hear it; I may even have said I was happy
for the French taxpayer. But I hurried to explain that in this present
case I could not be held responsible for the establishment or the
appointment of my officers. He gave me an instruction to reduce
this top-heaviness at once. This I may say was no easy task. Apart
from other things there were considerations of a man's remuneration
to be taken into account, the very core, the raison d'être of mercenary
soldiering, one must assume, although oddly enough this is not always true—not to mention loss of prestige, etc. But I did it. Not
without some soul-searching, but I did it. Naturally it left some ill
feeling among those who were summarily demoted in this distressing
manner, and one or two of these demotees, understandably, preferred to end their contracts then and there as a result. I cannot say
I blamed them.

There was still no word about Simon Donaldson and Ted MacKay.
The Major took the matter up vigorously with Etat Major who came
back with the news that two of my unit's white soldiers had deserted
across the border into Northern Rhodesia on May 8. An abandoned
jeep had been found at Kipushi. The number on the jeep was 234.
This, they said, must be my two men. But unfortunately it wasn't.
Our jeep was number 236. This was not conclusive because number
234 was also on my strength. But for two men to make a journey
in a jeep from northern Katanga to the bottom of Katanga, a distance
of some eight hundred kilometers, without being observed by anybody was, in my view, highly improbable. My anxiety increased.
So did the major's. Like the good leader he was, he arranged a special
interview for me with the C-in-C, Colonel Crèvecoeur, immediately.

I was ushered into the presence at Etat Major the next morning.
At the meeting I stressed my deep concern as to the fate of my two
men and the need for some immediate action. But it soon became
apparent to me that I was butting my head against a brick wall. The
old Congo hands at Etat Major already regarded the matter as closed.

If men will do these things, they implied with a shrug of their shoulders, they must bear the consequences. But that attitude was too negative for me to accept. Had they considered the possibility that the two men might even now be hiding somewhere, waiting for help? One was sick with malaria and the other was unable to make a long march. Assuming they had escaped from Nyunzu in 4 Commando jeep number 236, wasn't it conceivable, I asked, that they had run out of gasoline somewhere, had made their way to a Katangese outpost in the bush that was not in communication with base, and were expecting us to contact them? No, they said, it was not conceivable. The Colonel could not agree with me on any of the points I raised.

"I am sorry," he said, flatly, when I had quite finished. "You must face the facts. They will both be dead. In a year or so some missionary in the bush will report their death. News filters through to them via the tribesmen in their area. Eventually they hear everything this way. There is nothing you can do about it and nothing we can do. Just accept it as an unfortunate incident. Things like this have happened many times before. No doubt they will happen again. We know the Congo."

It all sounded horribly probable. In my heart I feared the worst. The thought that the two men had been captured by the Jeunesse, and had been killed, perhaps after the most hideous torture, haunted me. Was there nothing more I could do to find out? There was. I called on Colonel Bjorn Egge at United Nations Headquarters in Elizabethville. The Norwegian colonel was in charge of United Nations intelligence in Katanga. He was a smiling, boyish-looking man with a realistic approach to the problems besetting his organization at this time. He was known for his fair-mindedness and unbiased view of Katanga's independence. He began by congratulating me on my march, a compliment that came as a pleasant surprise. "Lucky for you you didn't hit the Jeunesse," he said. I agreed. But as far as helping with my present problem was concerned he regretted he could do nothing. Yes, he had heard all about the disappearance of the two men and if anything was reported to him he would let me know at once. He would warn all U.N. units immediately to make exhaustive enquiries in their areas and he would let me know the minute he received any information. I admired Colonel Egge. With hindsight I wish that he had been in overall command of the U.N.

operation in Katanga. He was a first-class soldier with a firm grip on both the military and political situations in Katanga at the time. He had an easy manner and could speak to both sides with authority, using the light touch. If anyone could have mediated successfully between the Independent State of Katanga and the United Nations peacekeeping forces it was he.

I returned to Shinkolobwe despondent. Two or three days later I received a message from Etat Major. A Dutch missionary in the Kiambi area had reported that a single jeep had been seen on May 7 on the road from Nyunzu to Kiambi. Kiambi was a small town two hundred kilometers due south of Nyunzu and a principal crossing place over the river Luvua on the main road to Manono. But instead of crossing the river to go on to Manono the jeep had turned east in the direction of Kapona and Baudouinville.

I contacted Etat Major at once. They confirmed the message and indicated that with this new information the matter could now definitely be closed.

"But why so?" I asked, perplexed. "What did this mean?"

"Why" they said, amazed at my ignorance, "don't you realize— they took the road to Kalamata! They headed straight for the enemy. The headquarters of the Baluba cartel is at Kalamata!"

The news stunned me. They took the road to Kalamata! God help them. I could not believe it. What in heaven's name had possessed them? But at least now that I knew, I was able to do something about it. I immediately called the men together and told them the latest news from Etat Major. I suggested we should mount a four-jeep fighting patrol, make Kiambi our base, and then go into Kalamata, seize some prisoners, and find out the truth one way or another. Subsequent action would depend on what we found out.

An old soldier spoke up. He was one of the officers I had been forced to demote but I don't think that influenced him in any way. The two men were obviously dead, he said. Too long a time had elapsed since they went missing. What I was now proposing was to risk the lives of another sixteen men for no good reason. The patrol would in all probability be surrounded by thousands of Jeunesse and no matter how brave or well-armed we might be we would be overwhelmed and end up losing our lives as well. He didn't think it was a good plan, but could offer no alternative.

"With respect, sir, why don't you call it a day? We know how you feel but you've got to face it—it's three weeks since it happened. They've had it." There was a general murmur of agreement. The men seemed to think that it was hopeless. But I thought otherwise and decided to swim upstream.

"Alright, now you've heard both sides of the story. Who'll join me to look for them?" Nearly everybody in the hall jumped to their feet. "I will, sir!" My main problem was who to leave behind.

I needed the permission of Major Falques. There was nothing impetuous or ill-considered about *mon major*. He wanted a written appreciation first, supported with a plan, every detail of the proposed action, and a nominal roll of the men taking part. In nineteen *exemplaires*, need I add. He gave his approval swiftly after studying the plan, and made a few professional suggestions to improve it. Where's your reserve? Make sure you leave some men at Kiambi . . . you never know. He agreed it was a necessary operation but warned me I was on my own if we got into trouble. It was not his intention to reinforce failure. *Bonne chance, mon capitaine!*

I chose the men carefully. It was rather like picking a school first team; many of those not chosen were going to be very disappointed. In my jeep, which would lead, I would have Des Willans and Frank Hastie, and a man named Vermuelen, who, despite his Flemish-sounding name, was an Englishman, a Geordie from Newcastle to be exact. He had gained a considerable reputation as an expert tracker, the result of many years service as a game ranger in the Luangwa Game Reserve in Northern Rhodesia. All the men were volunteers and the cream of the unit, including one man, commonly referred to as Holy Joe, who sometimes conducted drumhead services on Sundays and who said he would give the men a decent Christian burial when we found them. Despite this somewhat negative attitude I was glad to take him. He was a brilliant soldier.

We prepared meticulously for the patrol, checking every item of equipment several times over and leaving nothing to chance. Once we left Shinko we would be entirely on our own, not even in radio contact with Major Falques, whom we now regarded with respect as Big Roger. If you fear your leader, have respect for him, and admire him at the same time, you may be sure there is very little wrong with him. We left base with a flourish of trumpets and tremendous hope of success in our hearts, despite all the portents. We made Manono that night and reported to Captain Protin, the local Commandant de Place. He was extremely helpful and offered me some Katangese soldiers commanded by a Belgian adjudant to man the base at Kiambi. They would form my reserve. I accepted with gratitude. André Protin, apart from being as handsome as a film star, was that rare specimen, a staff officer with a thorough understanding of the needs of the fighting man.

The next day we hit the heavy white sand on the road out of Manono and our speed dropped to fifteen kilometers in the hour. The glare of the sun reflected off the white sand was fierce enough to melt the eyeballs, but there was instant relief when at long last we got to the river. The Luvua ran over half a mile wide at this point, just south of Kiambi, fast and deep, taking all manner of vegetation downstream with it. There was only one way wheeled traffic could cross the river and that was by ferry, a pontoon lashed on top of five or six steel boats driven by an asthmatic diesel engine. I noted that the nearest Katangese troops were stationed at an electricity generating station at a place called Piana Mwanga situated about thirty miles upstream, in case we might have need of them.

Once more we crossed the Luvua River in the knowledge that we were entering enemy territory and would be grossly outnumbered even though we had superior fire power. We motored slowly into the deserted village of Kiambi late that afternoon. It looked exactly what it was, a village in no-man's-land. We ground our way slowly up the deserted main street past boarded up shops and stores that had been closed for almost a year. We halted next to a hand-operated petrol pump, its glass smashed and its handle missing. From the store behind it an old Greek woman shuffled out in carpet slippers to meet us. She was almost completely wrapped in a black woolen shawl, despite the heat. If she was surprised or glad to see us she didn't say so. One of my men, a Katangese Cypriot, talked with her. The business was closed, she said, but she maintained the premises with her husband, who was away at the minute, against the day when peace would return to the country. Yes, of course she was lonely, but quite safe here. Why would anybody want to harm an old lady? It was well known in the Congo that the Greek traders, Cypriots mostly, who ran most of the country stores were neutral in tribal conflicts and left alone to supply both sides.

When I told her we would like to spend the night there she gave us the run of her house and let us use the kitchen. But please, we must be careful with her fresh water supply, which came from rainwater that she collected off the tin roof into a concrete butt. I supposed she was worried because the dry season had begun and there hadn't been any rain for over a month. But it wasn't that. The water butt contained a twelve-foot snake! To this day I have never figured out why she let it stay there unless its presence was intended to prevent pilfering. Apparently it was house-trained, or the equivalent, and came out at night. As her's was the only drinking water supply for miles around I kept the little secret from my men. What they didn't know wouldn't harm them, I supposed. No, she could not remember seeing a Jeep with two white men in it about three weeks ago. No, she had no information of the Baluba, she said, avoiding our eyes, but she could tell us the road to Kalamata was closed and had not been used for over six months. It had been the main road to Kapona and then Baudouinville before the war but now . . . She sighed deeply at the stupidity of men. What was it all about? she asked, with a shrug.

She showed us two large bare rooms on the first floor of the house. We laid out our kit on the bare floorboards and put down our blanket for the night. Our Greek prepared an evening meal while the rest of us unwrapped our weapons and cleaned them for the dash into Kalamata the next day. We would leave just after dawn.

The poster of Mr. Moise Tshombe, President of the Independent State of Katanga. It said, "Il souffre pour nous. Soyez digne de lui." He suffers for us (in Coquilhatville prison.) Be worthy of him.

Captain Alistair Wicks, second in command of 4 Commando, a gentle man and a fine officer.

Volunteer Pat Kirton, a clean-limbed blonde giant, a typical soldier of fortune of this time.

Lt. Issy Bernstein, previously of the Israeli army, one of the hardest men in 4 Commando.

Building the road near Pweto. When the mud road collapsed it had to be rebuilt with logs sawn from nearby trees.

Bogged down near Pweto. Torrential rain on the laterite surface made the road impassable to our convoy of fifty-one 5-ton trucks.

The bush where we lost Vol. Alec Auchterlonie.

4 Commando HQ at Nyunzu. R to L, Capt. Mike Hoare, OC 4 Commando, 2 Lt Simon Donaldson, Vol. Ted MacKay, Vol. Frank Hastie, Lt. Ian Coull, Vol. Claude Chanu, and the unit MO, Dr. Donnelly.

Volunteer Des Willans, the toughest soldier in 4 Commando. The man who hacked our way through the bush from Nyunzu to Niemba.

2nd Lt. Simon Donaldson, a genuine adventurer and firm believer in the rightness of Mr. Tshombe's cause.

"Holy Joe." The shepherd who cared for the souls of the little black sheep who'd lost their way.

The iron bridge over the river Lubilashi seen from the Kalamata side. It was here that Simon and Ted were overwhelmed by the enemy.

Speedy Donaldson, Simon's father, a millionaire mining magnate and a veteran soldier.

Phyllis Hoare, Mike's wife, armed with a Baluba bow and arrow, at Elizabethville airport.

Major Roger Falques, a distinguished French army officer with over twenty-two years continuous active service in Indo China and North Africa.

Kalamata seen from the air during the search for Simon and Ted.

Adjudant Edouard Lambrette, an officer in the Katangese Army. An ardent believer in the greatness of Katanga, his country, and an enthusiastic supporter of Mr. Tshombe.

A Greek mercenary soldier with Speedy Donaldson and Mike Hoare at Kalamata the day we found Simon's jeep.

Simon's Jeep no. 236. The Greek and a French mercenary who comforted Speedy Donaldson in Kalamata, with Adj. Lambrette and Mike Hoare.

Speedy Donaldson and Mike Hoare in Kalamata with Simon's Jeep no. 236.

The push to Mwenge. The Jeep recovered from an elephant trap fifteen feet deep, spiked with bamboo stakes. The driver, an Italian officer, died from his wounds.

8

The Road to Kalamata

IT was too hot to sleep and the mosquitoes stung abominably. An hour before dawn we rose and got moving again. My plan was to leave just after dawn and cover the seventy kilometers to Kalamata at top speed. We would stop a short distance from the village and make our approach on foot as stealthily as we could.

We left Kiambi just as the sun was rising, the four jeeps closed right up. I led. The windshields had been removed and we had placed sandbags on the hoods for protection and as a rest for our light machine guns. Less than eight kilometers down the road we came to a roadblock, a massive tree felled across the road. This was more or less what I had expected. We went round this through the bush with great care, watching out for mines, the obvious tactic, but not really expecting them. It was unlikely that the Baluba would be that sophisticated. Not yet, anyway. Nor did I expect ambush. Nobody could possibly have known we were going to use this road, not even the old Greek woman, whom I had made sure had been told we were headed for Nyunzu.

On the other side of the tree Vermuelen crouched on his hands and knees and began examining the left-hand side of the road. He signaled me to look at something he had found. He leaned forward and blew gently on the sand. The small leaves and other debris lying on the surface drifted away lightly to disclose the unmistakable marks of a jeep tire, the herringbone pattern plain to see. He checked again a few yards farther on and picked up the spoor once more. The man was an expert. This was encouraging; we were on the right track without any doubt.

We pushed on down the deserted road at top speed and saw no sign of man nor beast for the next thirty kilometers. Nothing stirred. The countryside was absolutely deserted. The silence was oppressive and charged with foreboding. The branches of the trees met over the road, throwing crisscross patches of sunlight and shade ahead of us, making observation difficult. The tunnel effect was disturbing and made it hard to focus. A turnoff to the right said Piana Mwanga. I looked at my map. That must be the road leading to the hydroelectric plant, which could also be approached from south of the river. I ignored it. We raced through Kashimba, a small village with huts on both sides of the road. It was deserted and looked as though it may have been vacated recently. The remains of wood fires outside several huts said it all. Now we were only fifteen kilometers from Kalamata.

My map was on a scale of 1:200,000, 1 centimeter to 2 kilometers, and was fairly accurate, but naturally on that scale not very detailed. But it showed clearly that there was a fork in the road about two kilometers this side of Kalamata, the upper prong leading into the village, the lower bypassing it entirely. We went hell for leather for the fork, lurching round the corners of the track in the heavy sand, the dense foliage muffling the sound of our motors. Here was the fork. I held up my hand. We closed up, dismounted, and went forward on foot. The alternative was to scream into Kalamata all guns blazing and then find ourselves surrounded by thousands of Jeunesse, who would materialize from nowhere once they realized we were on our own. The Baluba were not fools. They must be anticipating some reaction such as this on our part and have prepared a plan in advance. A single tree dropped on the track behind us would be enough to trap us. This was a time for stealth and caution.

I posted Des Willans and Frank Hastie two hundred yards ahead of us as forward scouts. The rest of the patrol strung out along the sides of the track, tactically, the jeeps bringing up the rear, closed right up fender to fender, driving as quietly as they could. Three hundred meters behind came my two rear scouts, looking back, always looking back. The deep sand slowed us down and blanketed any noise we made. I held up my hand. We halted. We listened hard for the usual sounds of village life, dogs barking, women calling, children crying; smelt the air for wood smoke and cooking; looked above the village for kite hawks and wheeling birds, which would have told us something. There was nothing. Not a damned sound.

Very strange. Now we used hand signals. Not a word was spoken. My heart was thumping as I caught sight of some thatched roofs about two hundred meters away. These must be the outskirts of the village. Safety catches were off. Suddenly Hastie raised his hand and signaled for us to advance at the double. As we came up to him he pointed to an object on the left side of the track. It was an effigy of a man. On the right side was another. Both effigies were stuffed with straw and made up to look like soldiers. The one on the left was much bigger than the one on the right and on its head it wore a black iron cooking pot. The smaller one had one made from earthenware. The effigies were horrible, evil-looking things, radiating dread. They looked as though they had been placed there to guard the entrance to the village.

I signaled to Da Silva to come up. He was a Portuguese who had lived all his life in Katanga and knew the rural Baluba intimately. He examined the effigies. "Traditional," he whispered. "The witch doctors have placed these here as a warning. They are telling strangers not to enter the village. But worse than that Captain. I'm sorry to have to say it but this can only mean one thing . . . our men are dead, and this is probably where they died. Look! That one is made to look like Simon, much taller than the other and wearing a black pot to resemble Simon's black beret. Don't you agree?"

Well, maybe I did. But it could also be a coincidence, couldn't it? And in any case we must not let our minds be influenced by mumbo jumbo of this sort. An effigy might scare the pants off a primitive Maluba but it ought to mean zero to us. Let's go. We pushed on with renewed caution.

Now we could see the village quite clearly. It was enormous, with row on row of huts laid out in ordered squares, but still no sign of any living soul. As we came round the last bend Willans suddenly threw himself on the sand and opened fire at the same time. The rest of us deployed and ran forward abreast of him and took up firing positions. There! Two black men were making a dash for the bush! Hastie raced off at an angle and fired in front of them on automatic, ripping up the track with bullets. They stopped. They were trapped. Both of them spun round and raised their hands. They were the only people there!

The bloody village was deserted after all. It was a hideous anti-climax. We went through the huts systematically to see if any old people had been left behind, the usual heartless custom in tribal conflicts in this part of the world. The very old were a hindrance in evacuations such as this, considered to be expendable and just left behind to die. But there was not a soul. More than three thousand people had just disappeared into the bush. It seemed fairly certain the place had been abandoned about three weeks previously, and judging by the remains of cooking fires, water in pots, and the amount of manioc lying in the huts the villagers must have been in a great hurry to go. We patrolled the length and breadth of the place and found nothing.

I told Willans to tie the prisoners to a stake and to guard them. Da Silva questioned them in Chiluba, the language of the Baluba, which he spoke fluently. Yes, they were Maluba. No, they didn't live here. They had just this minute arrived in Kalamata. They were businessmen. They came from Kiango, a village across the river. They had walked. No, they did not know why the village was deserted. It was a surprise to them too. No, they knew nothing of the two men we were looking for. They thought the villagers had gone into the bush to escape from Tshombe's army. They seemed to be telling the truth.

Meanwhile Vermuelen was examining the beaten track leading up to the chief's hut. Now he showed me where a jeep had turned in a complete circle in front of it. From the deeper indentation of the outer wheel marks it looked as though the jeep had been in a hurry to turn around. Or perhaps it had been very heavily loaded on one side. Vermuelen followed the tracks on foot until they led out of the village on to the road for Kapona. "Mount!" I shouted. "Follow me." And we pushed on down the road, taking the two prisoners with us.

Twelve kilometers further on we approached a small village called Kiungu. It was strung out on both sides of the road and deserted just like Kalamata. Once more we picked up the jeep tracks. Throwing caution to the wind we sped on as fast as we could, wondering what lay ahead. I was half-expecting, half-hoping we would find the jeep abandoned on the side of the road. If Simon and Ted had run out of petrol they would have had to leave the jeep and walk. It was a possibility. The road began to drop steeply and I could see there was some sort of valley ahead. I studied the map as we dashed along. That would be the Lubalashi River on our right. Now we were running parallel with it. It was a torrent of white water over fifty meters wide, dropping steeply and dashing through rocks and fallen trees at a ferocious seven or eight knots. I hardly had time to think about ambush when the road took a sudden turn right and we skidded to a dead halt. Right in front of us was a massive iron bridge. It was over thirty meters long and three meters high. We stopped on the brink. Every plank that had formed its roadway had been ripped out and carried away. Only the gray steel girders, which were massive and indestructible, were left standing.

No motor traffic had used this bridge for months, that much was certain. Pedestrians could still clamber across the iron girders fairly easily, but for vehicles there was no way over, nor any means of crossing farther upstream or downstream. Furthermore I was satisfied the jeep could never have been manhandled across that torrent of water. From the look of those vertical banks, six meters high in places, and the speed of the river, I would say that was totally impossible. Once more Vermuelen examined the track. Here, he said. This is where Simon's jeep stopped. And here you can see it returning in the direction of Kalamata. He was right. If the tire marks were those of Simon's jeep then it was still this side of the river. A few of us made our way across the bridge, hand over hand, and examined the ground on the other side. There were no tire tracks there.

My plan was now to go back slowly along the road to Kalamata and examine each village thoroughly. Perhaps we might find some clue, some piece of uniform or equipment, a water bottle perhaps, something that might indicate the men had passed this way. At Kiungu the tire marks disappeared completely, as the ground was rock hard, but by the side of the road, about ten yards into the bush, I noticed a small square of white cloth hanging limply from a long, thin bamboo pole, rather like an Indian prayer flag. I knew what that signified in this part of the world. A burial place. We dismounted and made our way to a clearing in the middle of which we found two graves, recently dug. The earth looked as though it may have been turned about three weeks previously. My pulse began to race. Could this be them after all? Perhaps this was journey's end. I hoped to God it wasn't. And logically it seemed unlikely. If Simon and Ted had been killed here, wouldn't the Baluba have thrown the bodies into the fast-flowing river? Maybe, but we must not ignore the graves even so. There was no alternative but to exhume the bodies.

I sent for Jock Hastie, remembering he had been an undertaker in his civilian life, and sought his opinion. Did I want a quote? I said no, get on with it. Frank said he was more used to putting people under the ground than digging them up, but he set to without a murmur. He thought it would take about two hours; the ground was baked hard. The remainder of us went through the village hut by hut. We found nothing. An hour later Frank called me to look at what he had found. About a meter and a half down he had unearthed two cooking pots and two drinking mugs. This was a sign, he said, that the graves were those of Baluba. He also thought it likely that we would find the bodies had been buried in the sitting position, which was the normal custom in this part of Africa. Should he go on? I said yes. We must be absolutely certain the graves did not contain Simon and Ted.

Another hour later Frank came across a black head and a black hand. Young men, he would say, after a little examination. He went a bit further and asked me if I would like to examine the corpses with him. He thought they had been buried about a month. To my surprise there was a total absence of that foul smell of putrefaction which, once experienced on the battlefield or elsewhere, will last you the rest of your days. Didn't I think he ought to go on and see if they had died of gunshot wounds? He was quite prepared to do it, there was nothing squeamish about Frank. But for my part the ghoulish job was turning my stomach and I had had more than enough. I said no. There was no point in disturbing the graves any more than we were obliged to now that we had found out what we wanted to know. I asked Frank to fill them in. We left them as we found them. It was a horrible, gruesome job.

We returned to Kalamata, baffled. Vermuelen was convinced he could see traces of a jeep track leading out of the back of the village in a northerly direction, toward a village called Nyandwe. The grass was more than head high here and the track so obscured I decided against following it. That was ideal ambush country. In any case the day had practically gone and I would have to find a strong point for the night pretty soon. I studied the map and thought somewhere near the *bac*, the ferry across the river, might be the safest. With the river behind us we would have only one front to defend and there would be good fields of fire on all sides. When we got there I re-membered the *bac* clearly as the main crossing point of the river on my trans-Africa journey some years before. But now it was derelict. It raised a pleasant moment of nostalgia even so.

During the night I decided there was still one more thing we could do. If Simon and Ted had been captured in Kalamata it was probable that they had been taken to a village the other side of the bridge where the Baluba would think the Katangese Army could not follow them. The map showed there was a village named Kasongo about seven kilometers from the bridge. That would be the logical one they would go to. We must visit it.

At dawn we returned to the bridge over the Lubalashi. I left six men to guard the jeeps and took the rest on a patrol to Kasongo. After covering five kilometers, mostly uphill, and seeing nothing on the road or in the bush, I began to wonder if this operation was wise. I was now perilously thin on the ground in two places and logically there was nothing to suggest that Kasongo would reveal any more than the other villages we had examined. I called it off and returned to the bridge.

We had another look at Kiungu and a final look at Kalamata and then called it a day. There was nothing more we could do. Summing up the results of the patrol I was forced to admit that they amounted to nothing more than a strong possibility that the tire marks we had seen leading from Kalamata to the bridge were those of Simon's jeep. Just that, nothing more. It was disappointing. We were in fact no further forward in solving the riddle of their disappearance. I turned the prisoners over to André Protin at Manono and, somewhat down-cast, headed for home.

I reported fully to Major Falques who suggested I should take a couple of days off and visit the C-in-C and Colonel Egge once more. Accommodation in hotels in Elizabethville at this time was scarce so that the best I could get was a room at a local monastery. The room turned out to be a cell but this was quite comfortable and suited my state of mind admirably. In any case I had always wanted to see what it was like to live like a monk and rather fancied myself in a brown soutane with hood.

Just after reveille I heard a raucous voice from the cell next-door singing a bawdy song in English. The voice was strangely familiar. It turned out to be that of Bertie Palmer. We met in the passage outside. He greeted me like a long-lost cousin, which threw me for a moment seeing that I was the one responsible for his arrest. He wore no badges of rank, on a uniform that was unexpectedly clean and smart for the Palmer that I remembered.

He answered my unspoken inquiry. Yes, he was out on a form of bail and today was D day. His court-martial was to begin at ten o'clock that morning. He was being defended by an eminent Belgian counsel, Maître somebody or other, whom he had retained at enormous cost. *Pas de probleme*, he was certain he would get off. Not if there was any justice in the world, I muttered. He knew damn well he was as guilty as all get out, but he was confidence itself. He gave me a lift as far as Etat Major where I had an appointment with the C-in-C. Later I would visit Colonel Egge. Once I had reported fully to both of them I would feel that I had done everything it was possible for me to do regarding the disappearance of my two men.

But the day held two big surprises for me. The first had to do with Bertie Palmer. Unbelievably he was acquitted! Palmer's counsel had addressed the court: "My client wishes to make a statement before his trial commences. The statement is in connection with the death of Patrice Lumumba. My client will state that he was present at the time of Lumumba's death in January of this year and has certain new and important evidence to bring to the notice of this court which could have serious international repercussions to the detriment of the Independent State of Katanga." The court agreed to receive and consider this statement before Palmer's trial began. They would adjourn for an hour for this purpose.

In order that you might appreciate the enormity of Palmer's suggestion, I am going to recount briefly for you the known facts and some of the myth surrounding the death of Patrice Lumumba at the end of January or beginning of February 1961.

Toward the end of 1960 the recently formed Democratic Republic of the Congo was in a state of utter confusion, and in many places total anarchy. The first prime minister of the Congo, Patrice Lumumba, had been deposed and was imprisoned in Leopoldville. President Kasavubu had shown himself unable or unwilling to act decisively in the political sphere. Colonel Mobutu, the Army Chief of Staff, had filled the vacuum thus created by establishing an administration made up of college students. For the moment this action had saved the country from sliding into irretrievable chaos. But it was generally thought that Mobutu had not been tough enough, so that soon he came to be labeled one of the weakest strongmen in history—a judgment later years were to see reversed with a vengeance. However, Kasavubu and Mobutu both agreed that it was imperative to keep Lumumba in prison indefinitely and to prevent his return to power at all costs. It was thought at this time that a return to power by Lumumba was the policy favored by the United Nations and also the United States. Lumumba's return would certainly have meant renewed civil war and, of course, death for Kasavubu and Mobutu.

Their original intention was to imprison Lumumba near Matadi at the mouth of the Congo River, but that fortress was found to be too unreliable. Tshombe was then approached to take over the prisoner but flatly refused to have anything to do with the matter. Kasavubu then appealed to Albert Kalonji, the Baluba leader of the Mining State of South Kasai, to become Lumumba's jailer. Kalonji was agreeable to this, particularly as Lumumba had been responsible for the shedding of much Baluba blood three or four months previously. A quid pro quo offered to Kalonji was that Lumumba would be tried for the genocide of the Baluba people.

On January 17, 1961, Patrice Lumumba, Joseph Okito, the former Deputy Speaker of the Congolese Parliament, and Maurice Mpolo, a former Minister for Youth and Sports, were sent by plane from Leopoldville to Kalonji's capital at Bakwanga. During the flight all three prisoners were brutally beaten up by their Congolese guards.

When the plane, a DC 3, arrived at Bakwanga, the pilot found it impossible to land because the landing strip had been obstructed by drums placed along the runway. He then decided to fly on to Elizabethville, but whether that decision was taken on his own initiative or on orders from Leopoldville is not known. In any event Lumumba is reported to have arrived at Elizabethville in a near-dead condition. Tshombe was thus placed on the horns of a dilemma. Much as he did not wish to be saddled with the responsibility of imprisoning Lumumba, neither did he wish to return him to Kasavubu and take the chance of his assuming power once more. The three prisoners were taken to a villa outside of town.

From that moment on the fate of Lumumba and his two aides is not known for certain and lies in the realm of conjecture. The Katangese government's version of events was that the three prisoners were taken to a farm near Mungulunga in the Dilolo department of Lulua Province and imprisoned in an outhouse. The outhouse walls were made of sandstone and the room they were held in measured five meters by three meters. They were guarded by fifteen gendarmes commanded by a Belgian, Captain Julian Gat.

A short while later the Katangese government announced that Lumumba and the other two had dug their way out of the outhouse, overpowered two guards, stolen their guns and a car, and escaped on February 10. On February 13 Minister of the Interior Godefroid Munongo announced that the bodies of Lumumba, Okito, and Mpolo had been found near Kasaji, near Mungulunga. They had been killed by local villagers, tribe not specified for their own safety. Patrice Lumumba's body was buried secretly near where he was killed, the exact place of his burial being unknown to this day.

The unofficial version ran like this. A day or two after Lumumba arrived in Elizabethville, Tshombe and two other Katangese cabinet ministers visited Lumumba in the villa in which he was being held just outside the city. A drunken orgy ensued during which Lumumba was beaten up by his guards for the amusement of his visitors. Because he was already in a very weakened state from the maltreatment he had received on the plane and before, he is said to have died under the blows. Okito and Mpolo, who had witnessed the murder, were then shot.

Finally, here is the U.N. version, being the findings of an official Commission of Inquiry, which were published on November 14, 1961. The report stated that the commission was of the opinion that Lumumba and his two lieutenants were killed at the villa on the day they arrived. It concluded: "In all probability the murder took place in the presence of Tshombe, Munongo, and Kibwe." It also said that Carlos Huyghe and Captain Gat, described as Belgian mercenaries, were involved in the actual killing of Lumumba. Lastly it declared that Munongo himself had plunged a bayonet into Lumumba's chest. It should be remembered that the Central Congolese government had refused the U.N. Commission of Inquiry permission to visit the Congo or Katanga. The U.N. report was described by Tshombe as completely false.

In passing, let me quote a passage from "Katanga Report" by Mr. Smith Hempstone, the distinguished Africa expert and Africa correspondent of the *Chicago Daily News* in those years:

Lumumba's death was, on the face of it, a crime. This should not be allowed to conceal the fact, however, that Lumumba was an erratic, incompetent, corrupt racist whose demagogic actions brought death and suffering to literally thousands of Congolese. He used his intelligence and diligence in the cause of evil and in the end, he was his own victim. If it was necessary for one man to die for the good of the Congo, the most logical candidate for this honor would have to have been Lumumba.

When the court reconvened the president of the court-martial declared that the case against Palmer had been adjourned sine die. Palmer in the meantime was free to go. He scooted off to the nearest bar where he proceeded to get himself fighting drunk. From that day to this I have wondered if Bertie was bluffing. The probability of Bertie Palmer being involved in the death of Lumumba was, in my opinion, not only remote but ludicrous. Would those in authority have risked using such a crass, egregious individual for such a nefarious undertaking, always supposing that Lumumba had in fact been murdered as was generally held? I couldn't see it, but one never knows. Stranger things have happened in the Congo. A deportation order was served on Palmer almost immediately afterward.

The second surprise was more fateful. I was lunching with Adrian Porter, the BBC correspondent in Katanga at that time, at Chez Felix, an excellent restaurant run by a Belgian. Felix did a memorable *steak au poivre* and still had a few bottles of my favorite red wine, Nuits de St. George. Adrian brought me a message. A gentleman staying at his hotel, the Leo Deux, said he would like me to call on him urgently. Could I visit him at the hotel at nine o'clock the following morning?

His name was Donaldson.

9

Mr. Donaldson Senior

A MIDDLE-AGED man in a Harris tweed jacket came forward to meet me as I entered the foyer of the Hotel Leo Deux at exactly nine o'clock the next morning. He spoke in clipped, dry tones.

"My name is Donaldson. You are my son's commanding officer?"

"Yes, sir. I was."

"Have you seen this?" He produced a newspaper cutting from the *London Daily Telegraph*. It gave an account of the disappearance of Simon and Ted. I read it.

"Well. What do you know about it?"

His brusque manner betrayed an anxiety that I could understand only too well. It aroused no reaction in me other than a very genuine sympathy. I suggested we sit down and have some coffee.

I gave him the whole story. It was extremely difficult to tell him exactly what had happened without causing him pain and I was as careful as I could be not to do that. But in the end I had to tell him the truth, that we were now forced to assume his son was dead. I described our patrol to Kalamata and the circumstantial evidence we discovered, which tended to confirm that view. I was sorry but I could not honestly hold out any hope. He heard me out without interruption. If I was expecting a normal reaction to that dreadful news I was to be surprised, and not for the last time, by this extraordinary man.

"Nonsense!" he exploded. "This isn't the first time Simon has been given up for lost. And I doubt if it will be the last. The boy's a born adventurer and a bloody nuisance at times. Two years ago we had half the French Navy out looking for him in the Bay of Biscay."

I said yes, I knew. Simon had told me about it. But this was different. He ignored the comment. Nothing, he continued, would convince him that there was no hope.

"Now listen to me," he said, rapping the table with the knuckles of his right hand. "This is probably what happened. He and MacKay must have run out of petrol somewhere between Kiambi and Baudouinville and have taken shelter in a native village. The blacks are looking after them. Simon is lame. I expect you know that. Neither of them would be able to walk far, but in due course they will make their way back to civilization one way or another. I'm certain of it."

"With respect, sir, do you know the country?"

"Same as Tanganyika, I expect," he said, curtly. "I know that very well. Should do, lived there for years. Bush is very much the same anywhere in this latitude. In any case Simon speaks Swahili fluently, you know that don't you? That'll help a lot."

I agreed it would in normal circumstances.

"Right then. The first thing to do is to organize some help for them. What can you suggest?"

I said I thought he should meet the C-in-C and Colonel Egge of the United Nations, the two officers with the greatest authority in Katanga. They were our best bet. We took a taxi to Etat Major. The C-in-C said he would see us immediately.

Colonel Crèvecoeur replied very formally to all the questions put to him by Mr. Donaldson. But after that he was brutally frank. "Your son is dead, sir. I regret there is nothing more we can do." Colonel Egge was more sympathetic but could offer no hope.

Mr. Donaldson had a two-day visa for his visit to Katanga and this expired the next day. I accompanied him to the airport. He was less anxious now that he knew the circumstances of Simon's disappearance, not that it made him any more congenial, but he made it clear that as far as he was concerned this was by no means the end of the matter. He intended to pursue it all the way. He inferred bluntly that in his view the affair was to some extent my responsibility as I was his commanding officer. I said yes, I agreed, that could be so. But after some thought I decided that the time had now come to take a less apologetic stance and to tell him the entire story, a vital part of which I had avoided so far in order not to hurt him. His refusal to accept that Simon was dead would make it easier for me.

I then told him that his son had disobeyed my last order, which was to fall in with the other men, and that he had gone off on his own with MacKay in an apparent attempt to reach Baudouinville, and that it was this action on Simon's part that had led directly to the tragedy. But the last thing I wanted was an argument about responsibility, which was pointless at this stage. I ended by saying that I felt a very deep sympathy for him and his family and that I was at his disposal and would give him all the help I could should he need me any further.

"I'll hold you to that," he said, sternly, and marched off toward the departure lounge.

Two weeks later I was in Durban on leave. I don't want to burden you with my private life but as it now forms a vital part of the story I must ask you to excuse me. I had known a beautiful young girl in Durban for the previous three years, during which the romance had blossomed into love despite my rather odd way of life and the fact that she was very much younger than I. From time to time we had discussed marriage without reaching any conclusions. A further complication was, from my point of view, that she was very much in demand, something which she confirmed from time to time by way of refined torture. Circumstances had not been altogether propitious either, as Phyllis had been working as an air stewardess with Central African Airways in Salisbury and this had meant long periods when I did not see her at all, which had also tended to slow down the marriage stakes.

But there is nothing like a spell of loneliness in the bush to quicken the sensibilities and make one appreciate the real things in life, the most important of which might easily be the finding of one's mate. So I had decided that as soon as I saw her again after my return I would make the proposal in the old-fashioned way.

A few evenings later I took her to dinner at the Causerie, a romantic restaurant in The Edward, one of Durban's most enchanting hotels. It was a beautiful evening and everything was completely right as we sat gazing upon the moonlit waters of the Indian Ocean, holding hands and listening to the strains of a dance orchestra in the background. *Le moment critique* had arrived. But to my astonishment my romantic intentions were summarily preempted.

"You have been messing around in the Congo too long!" she said, firmly, looking me directly in the eye. "Give me a straight answer. Will you marry me?"

"Now that you put it that way, yes I will," I replied, accepting the graceful proposal with a joyous heart and a straight face.

"By the way," I said, "just try this on for size. I just happen to have it on me."

I produced by magic an engagement ring from my waistcoat pocket. When she realized that she had beaten me to it by a short head her fury was spectacular. She cast around frantically for something heavy to crown me with. With unerring instinct she seized on a nearby bottle of wine. Fortunately it had a distinguished pedigree, a Mouton Rothschild, 1935, I seem to remember.

A week later we were married.

But my plans for the honeymoon were stymied and unexpected events placed me in an embarrassing predicament. Phyllis was at a travel agency, intent on booking two airline tickets to Mombasa, where we were to spend three weeks at the Nyali Beach Hotel, when fate intervened in the shape of a telephone call from Johannesburg. It was Mr. Donaldson.

"You remember you said I could rely on you for help in finding Simon?" he said, coming straight to the point. "Well, I've decided to take you up on that. I have chartered a private aircraft and I'm flying at once to Bulawayo and then Abercorn in Northern Rhodesia. You know Abercorn, don't you? It's at the bottom end of Lake Tanganyika. Same latitude as Lake Mweru. That will be my base, and from there I intend to fly all over northern Katanga until I find my boy. But I will need your help. You're the chap with the local knowledge. You must tell us where to look. Are you on?"

I was struck dumb. No use explaining my marital affairs to him at a time like this. I backed off a little.

"Do you think you can get Katangese permission to fly over their air space?" I asked. "They're very touchy about this sort of thing."

"Don't need it, old chap. I'm going to do it regardless, with or without permission. Better with, of course. Can you help there?"

"Certainly. I'll ring Carlos Huyghe tonight. I'm sure he'll be able to arrange everything."

"Right then. I'll meet you at Baragwanath Airport tomorrow morning at 1000 hours. ETD 1030. Make sure you are on time, won't you, we've a long way to go." He rang off. Feeling a little stunned I put the phone down. I had heard quite a lot about "Speedy" Donaldson in the two weeks since I first met him. He was not a millionaire mining magnate for nothing. He knew what he wanted and he invariably got it.

I raced round to the travel agency. Phyllis was waiting for the tickets, which they were making out even then.

"Hold everything, my lotus blossom," I said, gulping fresh air like a stranded whale. "Small alteration to our plans, my darling," I began, seizing her sword arm. "Scrub Mombasa! Horrible hot place at this time of the year. Can't imagine why I forgot that. Monsoon raging, mosquitoes biting, awful humidity—you'll hate it. I've thought of a much better place."

"Let me guess," she said, beautiful blue eyes brimming with excitement. "I know. Venice! You've always told me how wonderful it is." Heaven help me, I was getting in deeper. "Well . . . er . . . no . . . not exactly. I was really thinking more about . . . well, er . . . Elizabethville."

A woman's love is a many splendored thing. She agreed at once, subject only to one thing. Could she bring a bulletproof vest? She just happened to have one in her trousseau.

I arrived punctually at Baragwanath Airport, the civil airport for private aircraft on the Witwatersrand in those days, to find Mr. Donaldson waiting for me. He introduced me to Mr. Hans Haaroff and told me he was the senior pilot of the air charter company, and one of the most experienced and highly regarded aviators in southern Africa. I was relieved to hear it. He would need to be for the job in hand. The plane was a four-seater Cessna 310, a twin-engined job with wing pods. It had a range of 1500 miles, which was reassuring. I would hate to have to come down in Baluba territory from lack of fuel.

We flew via Bulawayo, Salisbury, and Ndola, a total distance of 1380 miles, making a night stop at Ndola, one of the principal towns in the northern Rhodesian copperbelt. We were to come down at Abercorn early the next morning. Abercorn was a small town just a few miles below the southern end of Lake Tanganyika in about latitude 9 degrees south, which was about the same as the adjoining area we were going to search. We made a perfect landing on Abercorn's wide red earth airstrip, refueled, and took off due west for Katanga at once. Our first task was to search the entire length of the road from Nyunzu to Kiambi, just to make absolutely certain Simon's jeep was not broken down somewhere along it.

I sat in the front seat with Hans and assisted him wherever I could by recognizing towns and villages and rivers. We overflew Pweto at the northern end of Lake Mweru, where we had suffered those agonizing days with the ill-fated convoy, and then flew along the River Luvua, toward Kiambi, at about five hundred feet. From there we went north circling low each time we came to a village on the side of the road. Nyunzu was about two hundred fifty air miles from Abercorn so we had a comfortable reserve of fuel. Our cruising speed was about 130 miles per hour. When we had satisfied ourselves there was nothing on the Nyunzu-Kiambi road we began the more important part of the search, which was the country between Kiambi and Kapona. Hans had gridded up his air map into tracks running west-east and then east-west. After we had flown over those we would then fly north-south and south-north over the same area. In this way we would be absolutely certain to cover every piece of the ground. Mr. Donaldson was sitting behind me, quietly.

"What exactly are we to look out for?" I asked.

"Simon will come out of one of these native huts and wave to us," he said, with disarming confidence.

We pressed on in total silence. We flew for hour after hour at five hundred feet, sometimes even lower, almost at stalling speed, banking and turning until I felt miserably air sick. But we saw nothing.

"What are the chances of being shot at around here?" asked Hans.

"Quite good, but it will only be small arms fire and the odds on being hit are negligible."

"Glad about that," said Hans. He was as solid and unflappable as a rock.

We returned to Abercorn for the night and started early again the next day, determined to fly even lower where necessary. This time we would concentrate on the villages in the Kalamata area. We approached from Kiambi and flew down the road we had taken on our patrol. There was the tree still lying across the road, there was the turnoff to Piana Mwanga, and there was the entrance to Kalamata. We were so low I could even see the two effigies. We circled lower and lower almost touching the roof tops. The surging of the plane's shadow across the thatched roofs seemed to mesmerize me. Nothing else stirred.

We flew on to Kiungu. It was exactly as we had left it. Then the iron bridge over the Lubalashi, the river still thundering under it.

Now we were over Kasongo, the village we had not reached on our patrol. As we flew over it at zero feet a black man dressed in a bright blue shirt and trousers came out of a hut and waved! My heart leapt. We circled again and again as low as we could but he just stood there looking up. He seemed dazed and made no further attempt to communicate with us. That was a disappointment, but Mr. Donaldson thought that if there was one man there there may be others. Perhaps Kasongo was inhabited after all.

We flew down the Luvua again and then up it for the last time. We had covered every track on the grid Hans had prepared. No spot on that map had been overlooked.

"Once more for luck," said Hans as we made the final pass over Kiambi, Kalamata, and Kasongo. As the three villages dropped away behind us Hans said quietly, "I'm afraid that's all we can do from the air, Mr. Donaldson. Shall we head for Abercorn?" Mr. Donaldson grunted his agreement from the back seat.

We flew steadily southeastward for a few minutes, gaining height as we went. I felt a very deep sorrow for Mr. Donaldson at this moment. Surely, I said to myself, this is the awful moment when he has to come face-to-face with the inescapable truth and acknowledge it: Simon must be dead. I turned in my seat to offer him my heartfelt sympathy, expecting to find him stricken with grief. He wasn't. He was reading a novel by Hammond Innes and eating some sandwiches. I never said a word. I had misjudged the moment and possibly the man. "Interesting book," he said. "Knew the author. We were up at Cambridge together."

During the night stop at Ndola we planned the next step. Another visit to Elizabethville was essential but it was not possible to use the Cessna. We would have to arrive by scheduled airline in the normal way. Mr. Donaldson, whose resources were formidable, was planning to bring his big guns into action.

"Do you know the British Consul in Elizabethville?"

"Mr. Denzil Dunnett? Yes. I have met him. Very helpful chap. I'm sure he'll do whatever he can."

"What about the press corps? Do you think you could arrange a conference for me? I want the world to know about this."

I was being obliged to assume the role of aide-de-camp!

"Well that's not really my line, but I can put you in touch with a journalist friend of mine, John Latz. He's a stringer for AP. He'll certainly be able to arrange something for you. Why, what have you got in mind?"

"If the Katangese government isn't prepared to do something about Simon I'm going to make sure the world knows how they treat people who volunteer to help them. And it won't do them a scrap of good."

Mr. Donaldson was on very firm ground there. The Independent State of Katanga had reason to be sensitive about its image world-wide, and the news that one of its army officers, albeit a mercenary soldier, had been abandoned without so much as an official enquiry or an adequate search would react most unfavorably against them. As Simon was also a British citizen, Mr. Dunnett would be obliged to take more than a cursory interest in the affair.

I telephoned Phyllis in Durban and asked her to fly up to Eliza-bethville on a Sabena Boeing out of Johannesburg as soon as possible. I would get Carlos Huyghe to authorize her entry. She must meet me at the Hotel Leo Deux. At the same time I warned Mr. Donaldson that he could expect problems with the immigration authorities when he arrived. It was probably in the interests of many people to deny him entry. But I would meet him on arrival and do what I could.

I have found over the years that the ease with which a bona fide traveler can enter a Central African country is some indication as to its state of advancement. Petty officialdom in many Central African states at this time, and even now I am sorry to say, thrived on tyranny, some civil servants finding it necessary to pay themselves if only because their governments had failed to do so. The net result was that many of the small everyday transactions of life became intolerable.

I recall for instance trying to collect my mail one day at the Poste Restante counter at Elizabethville Post Office. There was a long queue, and when I finally got to the grille I was asked, quite rea-sonably, to show my passport as a means of identification. The clerk then took great delight in thumbing slowly through every page and questioning me on each entry and visa in it, which of course had nothing whatsoever to do with him. I presumed he wanted to dem-onstrate his authority in the hope that I would be blackmailed into dashing him a few francs to make certain I got my mail. As I was in uniform at the time I was able to let him know I could inform his superiors of his irregular behavior. It did the trick. How civilians managed I wouldn't know.

10

A Punitive Expedition

As anticipated, the immigration people refused to allow Mr. Donaldson to enter the country on his arrival at Elizabethville airport. I insisted that they should ring up Carlos Huyghe. Somewhat reluctantly Huyghe smoothed the way and arranged for Mr. Donaldson to be admitted, but only after warning him that publicity in connection with his son's disappearance would not be tolerated and that he must leave the country within seven days. Nice treatment, I thought, for a man whose son had been killed in the service of their country.

Phyllis arrived later that same day from Durban and we were installed briefly in the luxurious if ruinously expensive Hotel Leo Deux. That such a place should exist at all was a tribute to Belgian enterprise. The place was a veritable oasis, a little bit of Belgium dropped into the center of Africa. Its haute cuisine was justly renowned throughout the length and breadth of the continent for its variety and excellence. This was made possible largely by an air freight service, which flew into Elizabethville twice weekly from Brussels via the national carrier, Sabena. The dining room was always crowded and well patronized by local notables and dignitaries.

Mr. Donaldson wasted no time. He called on Colonel Egge and Mr. Dunnett at once. Meanwhile I asked John Latz to arrange a press conference tentatively for seven that evening. This was to have repercussions beyond our wildest imaginings. Then we visited Etat Major and asked to see the Commander in Chief. Unexpectedly we were shown in at once. The Colonel listened patiently to the story again, nodding sympathetically from time to time, and took notes. Strange, I thought to myself, it looks as though he may have had a change of heart. What I didn't know at that moment was that he was just about to be replaced as Commander in Chief by General Norbert Moke, a Katangese. After some deliberation he spoke.

"Perhaps I can help. What would you like me to do for you?"

Mr. Donaldson looked to me for a suggestion. I spoke up.

"Give me permission to organize a fighting patrol in strength. Let it stay in the field until we have found the missing jeep and proved conclusively the events which took place on May 7 in the Kalamata area."

He considered this for a moment and then handed me a signal pad.

"Write out whatever you need," he said, calmly. I was stunned. It was all going too well, too easily. Why this change of policy? And so suddenly. Perhaps the news of the intended press conference had already filtered through and caused second thoughts somewhere. It could only be that. This new initiative would put a stop to that, of course, and make the threatened publicity unnecessary. As I made out my list, the C-in-C and Mr. Donaldson chatted amiably.

The C-in-C examined my operational requirements.

"Two hundred men, six armored cars, an 81 mm mortar platoon, two light aircraft, a helicopter . . . What is this—are you going to start a war? Is this a fighting patrol or a punitive expedition?"

"Perhaps both," I said.

"Alright. I'm quite prepared to authorize it, but there is one very big problem which we have to solve first. That is the question of finance. You will appreciate that an expedition of this magnitude might cost the Katangese Government . . ."

Mr. Donaldson waved him down impatiently.

"Never mind what it costs, Colonel. Just send me the bill."

The C-in-C rang for his staff officer and issued a confirming order. He rose to indicate that the interview was over. He saw us to the door.

"Mr. Donaldson, I suggest you treat this operation with maximum security, and I must insist that you avoid the press. Meanwhile we shall keep in contact with you at your hotel as and when we receive any news."

Mr. Donaldson shook his head vigorously. This was not at all what he had in mind.

"I want your permission to accompany the column. You may not know it but I'm an old soldier. I was an officer in the South African Imperial Light Horse during the war. Matter of fact I was a captain. We fought in the Libyan desert. This sort of thing's nothing new to me."

Crèvecoeur looked doubtfully at him and then at me but gave in after a while.

"Very well then, but you must let us have a written indemnity against any accidents, wounds, illness—things like that which may occur now or later as a result of your action. One never knows. The State must be covered, you understand that?"

"Naturally."

Now that he was doing something positive, something personal and physical in the search for his son, Mr. Donaldson began to bloom. He seemed to grow taller and broader as I looked at him. In this moment I admired the man for his dogged determination and his unconquerable spirit. In no way was he prepared to accept the negative hand of bureaucracy in its refusal to authorize a search for his son. He had won his first battle.

On the strength of this victory we had an aperitif at a local bar and made plans for our sojourn into the field. I took him to the quartermaster's stores and got him kitted out as a soldier. Mr. Donaldson asked me to call him Speedy, the nickname his brother officers had christened him with in the North African campaign. In my opinion it didn't actually suit him. Bulldog would have been more like it. Or Terrier. Nevertheless I used it thereafter, but always with that slight hesitation one experiences when addressing one's old commanding officer or headmaster in a familiar way.

I said good-bye to Phyllis and for the week or so I would be away in the field I put her in care of the handsome Carlos Huyghe. Not without some mild trepidation, may I say. I warned him I was as jealous as a bandit and had a special long-range peashooter to deal with chaps that even so much as thought about taking liberties with my bride. It was the damnedest honeymoon.

The fighting patrol was to be assembled at Manono, the tin mining town just south of the River Luvua, the scene of heavy fighting against the Baluba some months before. Speedy and I flew up in a battered prewar DC 3, which bounced twenty feet off the grass strip on making its two landings. Once more Captain Protin had arranged everything magnificently. He paraded the patrol for my inspection. It consisted of one *groupe mobile* supported by a company of Katangese infantry plus a platoon of 81 mm mortars, all exactly as requested. The Ferret armored cars were not available but two light aircraft, Piper cubs, were ready and waiting on the airfield at Manono. Splendid. They would be ideal for the air reconnaissance, which would be essential. The *groupe mobile* was led by a young Belgian officer who had under his command several mercenary officers, some of whom had served in the ranks of the French Foreign Legion. I was glad to see that none of them could be described as *les affreux*. For liaison purposes a young Belgian adjudant was attached to my headquarters. His name was Edouard Lambrette, an energetic and vivacious character of about twenty-three who had been born and bred in Katanga and spoke several Congolese languages fluently, including Swahili and Chiluba. Like all the Belgian *colons* whom I met in Katanga he loved this country, his country, with a passion and knew its people intimately. He treated his Katangese soldiery with unaffected superiority, in much the same way I imagine a thirteenth century English nobleman might have treated his serfs. In their turn they respected him and followed him devotedly.

I began by sending Speedy Donaldson on an air reconnaissance of the entire area, accompanied by two of the Belgian commanders. This would familiarize them with the terrain we were going to search on foot. Once more I would use Kiambi as a forward base.

We set off the next day. The column, which was a formidable one, churned its way steadily through 160 kilometers of heavy white sand at an average speed of about twenty kilometers in the hour. Yet again the glare of the reflected sunlight seared the eyes and dulled the brain.

Lambrette traveled with me in my jeep. All the way he regaled me cheerfully with stories of life as it was lived in the old Congo Belge. It sounded like paradise. Passing through the scrub and low bush veld country just south of the Luvua River, near Kiambi, he showed me the exact spot where he had shot his first elephant. This was magnificent big game country, he said. Eland, kudu, buffalo, even carnivora roamed the country freely, and of course many of the lesser antelopes. But no rhino. (That came as no surprise to me; by the turn of the century I imagine rhino will be extinct in Africa.) Lion were classed as vermin, can you imagine that? he said.

But since independence those days had gone, he sighed, never to return again. Which was a damned shame, he continued with some emotion, switching to the political scene, because if left to run Katanga by themselves black and white Katangese could have created a great multiracial nation and made a famous success of it. He was convinced of it. Yes, they would have been a shining example to the rest of Africa, even the world. He felt keenly that this wonderful opportunity had been lost, largely, he said, because of interference by an ignorant American administration which knew nothing of Africa on the one hand, and the stupid United Nations which knew even less on the other. As a result, he argued, his birthright had been forfeited and the clock put back another twenty years.

I asked him why he and so many other Belgians were anxious to see Katanga as an independent sovereign country and not merely a province of the new Democratic Republic of the Congo. He replied that throughout its history Katanga had always been a separate nation. This was not surprising, he went on. Katanga was fundamentally different in many important respects from the other five provinces of the Congo. It was only the drawing of arbitrary boundaries on a map at some conference in Europe eighty years ago that had turned Katanga into a part of the Congo, a hodgepodge of over two hundred twenty different tribes. Geographically too Katanga and the other provinces were different. The Katangese terrain for a start was high and open, mostly ranch-type country unsuitable for agriculture, unlike the rest of the Congo. Then again the majority of Katangese spoke Swahili, all the other provinces spoke either Chiluba, Lingala, or Kikongo. The Katangese found it irksome and impractical to be ruled by a remote legislature in Leopoldville some two thousand five hundred kilometers away. Ethnically Katanga's people were entirely separate from the other tribes in the Congo as well. Did I not realize that the difference between the Katangese and the people of the Bas Congo was as marked as that between a Ukranian in Russia and a Flamand in Belgium? And you find the idea of sharing your vast wealth with the other provinces unattractive too, I suggested with a laugh. Yes, he said, he had to admit that didn't appeal to them much either.

The tragedy was, he went on, that their country had become a political football. Too many outsiders, many of them newly independent African states like Ghana, with no real knowledge of the country or its problems, were involved in deciding its future, for reasons that had nothing whatever to do with the Congo. Even the Belgians themselves had done much to force Patrice Lumumba on the Congo as its first prime minister—Lumumba, an ex–postal clerk who had to be taken out of prison, where he was serving a sentence for petty theft, in order to attend the very conference in Brussels which then brought him to power! And why? Because the Belgian government wanted a unitary state so that Belgium could perpetuate its control of the Congo, and Lumumba was the only politician whose manifesto would have permitted that policy.

He could see no happy ending for Katanga the way things were working out. As it turned out he was correct in his dismal forecast, but he didn't live to see it. He was killed in the communist-inspired rebellion that took place in the Congo three years later in 1964.

Lambrette was also very knowledgeable about the days of slave trading in the Congo. These had ended only about one hundred years ago, but the memories of them, he told me, had been passed down faithfully from generation to generation of Congolese. And I could imagine they would lose nothing of their terror in the retelling. But I was amazed when he said that in the first half of the nineteenth century over one hundred fifty thousand men, women, and children were captured each year in the Congo and shipped from ports on the west coast of Africa to become slaves in the New World. Altogether over seven and a half million people had been transported in this way from the Congo alone. And we must suppose an equally large number, if not more, must have been killed in the attacks on their villages in which they were captured, or on the harrowing journey to the coast which followed, roped up and manacled as they were to prevent escape. The whole story came alive for me when I realized that the tracks on which we were now traveling were, in many cases, the same as those used by the slave traders in the previous century.

We began, as before, at Kiambi. The old Greek lady was still there, wearing her carpet slippers as before, and I presumed still providing board and lodging for her twelve-foot pet. My plan for the patrol envisaged two phases. Phase one would be a systematic reconnaissance in force, every village within a twenty-five-mile radius of Kalamata was to be searched. The hills behind the villages were to be patrolled on foot. Prisoners would be taken and passed back to base swiftly for interrogation. Phase two would involve cross-ing the Lubalashi River with a fighting patrol and penetrating into Baluba-held territory for a distance of fifty kilometers. Air recon-naissance would be carried out daily.

We covered the villages from Kayumba in the north to Piana Mwanga in the south in the first three days, working our way slowly eastward. The going was rough and slow. The tracks soon petered out and became footpaths so that we had to dismount and go forward on foot, the vehicles grinding along behind us in bottom gear, their radiators boiling after the first few kilometers. At the end of the third day Speedy began to show signs of severe fatigue. He was dressed as a soldier and armed with a Vigneron submachine gun, which I had taught him how to use. He was tough as old boots and never complained once even though the heat was oppressive for twelve hours a day. But the monotonous diet of rice, sardines, and dry biscuits was beginning to get him down. He said one day in a rare spasm of lightheartedness that he preferred his meals at the Rand Club in Johannesburg. Not surprising, given that it is Africa's most prestigious club.

On the fourth day we entered a village, which was sparsely in-habited. It seemed strange to me that the villagers made no attempt to run, the usual reaction to a visitation by the Katangese Army. Now they stood silently by as the Katangese soldiers began to ques-tion them. Suddenly it dawned on me why they hadn't run—we were in the middle of a leper colony! But Lambrette didn't seem to mind. He chatted away cheerfully with one old crone whose nose had been eaten away completely, leaving only two gaping holes in her face. He held up her hands for me to see that she had no fingers, just the palms. He laughed. The man was incorrigible. Some of the younger lepers held their arms over their faces shyly. Great heavens, I thought, why should this be with all the medical knowledge at our disposal in this day and age? As we left Lambrette told me that leprosy was a comparatively rare disease in Katanga today, and that what we had here was not really full-blown leprosy, but more like something he called yaws. Yaws was not nearly so prevalent as leprosy, it seemed, but was still a living horror. As far as he knew there was no cure for it.

Each night we made camp in a deserted village. Speedy and I would sprawl on the sand in front of a huge log fire and chat about his days in the northern desert—Cairo, Alamein, Mersa Matruh, Tobruk, Benghazi, all those places he had served in—until it was time to turn in on our single blankets. I used to look at him in the firelight and wonder what the mental stresses and the physical strains of this ordeal were doing to him. The peace of the African night, our quiet conversation, and the remembrance of things past gave me the chance to get closer to him. The bush and the rigors of the patrol began to break down his ironclad reserve, just a little, but his shell remained impregnable. Even so I got to know him in those few days as a decent, straightforward, and honorable man, not by any means lovable, but upright and courageous. Unyielding though he was there was much to admire in him—his bulldog tenacity for one thing, that determination never to give in. Even in the face of grueling hours in the sun and the painful progress we were making from village to village, piling disappointment on disappointment, I never heard him complain once.

Over a quiet Scotch one evening as we sat around the log fire, pushing a heavy log into the blazing timbers from time to time to send a column of sparks high up into the black night air, he told me something of his forebears. His father was the famous Colonel James Donaldson who is still well known in Southern Africa. Colonel Donaldson was born in London in 1863. After his education in Edinburgh he joined the old Cape Mounted Rifles, and in 1881 he moved to Kimberley where he took part in the gold rush of 1882 at Devil's Kantoor. After working as a trader and a miner and a transport rider at Barberton, he finally settled on the Witwatersrand. Later he helped Sir Wools-Sampson form the Imperial Light Horse, becoming a Lieutenant Colonel during the Boer War. His enormous wealth came from the diamond fields of the western Transvaal, and some of this he invested in diamond exploration in Tanganyika. Before he died in 1940 he devoted over one hundred thousand pounds to the setting up of a trust for the education and advancement of blacks.

So now I knew how Simon came to be in Tanganyika and how it came about that he had learned to speak Swahili, an accomplishment that probably contributed in the end to his death.

I said good night to Speedy with the feeling that the next day would probably prove conclusive. We were to end our search at Kalamata. One column would start in the north from Kabwala, a fairly large place, and then approach Kalamata via Nyandwe, a village seven kilometers from it. A second column would enter Kalamata from the main road as we had done on our patrol previously.

Nyandwe proved to be nonexistent. This often happens in Africa. The fact that a village is boldly stated on the map is no guarantee that it will be there at all. Tribal conflicts, loss of grazing, bad harvests—these are some of the circumstances that cause whole villages to be abandoned and their inhabitants to migrate. Sometimes villages perish through sheer inability to cope with Mother Nature.

Speedy and I were with the northern column. Toward noon a red Very light shot up out of the bush ahead of us. This was a signal that the other patrol had found something of importance. We hurried toward them to find a group of Katangese soldiers milling round a jeep with much excitement. I looked at once for the number—it was 236 right enough! It was without any question Simon's jeep, still hidden in the head-high grass less than four kilometers north of Kalamata. The windshield and the tailgate were missing but otherwise it appeared to be complete. I examined it carefully for bullet marks or other damage, and bloodstains. There were none. Some men pushed the jeep back along the track to the village. We camped in Kalamata itself. Night fell. Phase one was over.

Speedy and I sat quietly by the firelight thinking our own thoughts and saying nothing. Taking a solid block of C ration cocoa Speedy pounded it up in a mess tin with the boss of an FN bayonet. He added some boiling water and then handed me half the brew. There was nothing really to say. There could be no doubt now that Simon and Ted were dead. Finding the jeep was conclusive. Whatever his emotions were in that sad moment Speedy kept them to himself. He was a very private man; stoicism was part of his nature. I made no attempt to sympathize with him. I felt instinctively that it would be the wrong moment to do so. But a Greek and a French soldier to whom Speedy had taken a great liking came over after a while and offered him a swig of cognac from their flask. He accepted it. Then with an awkward tenderness they put their massive arms around him and uttered their condolences in simple broken English, straight from the heart. This got to him. For a moment his defenses were down, but I could feel this act of compassion was satisfying some need he had denied himself in the belief that to accept sympathy was unmanly. He murmured his thanks and they withdrew, quietly, leaving him alone once more with his thoughts.

The following day Speedy went back to Manono in one of the light aircraft, and then on to Elizabethville in a local bus. He said he would try to get an extension of his visa if he could and would wait a few days for me. Perhaps I might have some more news for him.

I gave orders for phase two of the operation to begin.

11

The Solution

I MOVED my headquarters to the iron bridge over the Lubalashi River. Our first task was to reconstruct a roadway over the girders. This meant chopping down trees, dragging them to the site, and shaping the timbers crudely with axes. It took the infantry company a full day to do it. As soon as I saw that I would be able to get my transport across to the other side I made plans for the operation.

The infantry company less two platoons would surround Kasongo at dawn with the intention of capturing as many prisoners as possible. The *groupe mobile*, with two infantry platoons under command, would move on Mwenge, the chief place in this area, with the same intention. Mwenge, which was heavily populated, was to be reached via Tembwe and Kibongo and was about fifty kilometers distant. With speed the *groupe mobile* should be able to achieve complete surprise, but it was possible that one or two of the streams that crossed the road could hold them up for a while. If this happened their approach was almost certain to be known in Mwenge. It was a risk they must reckon with. It was unlikely they would find any more bridges destroyed. Air reconnaissance had revealed nothing in the way of obstruction on the road, but this information was to be treated with extreme caution as the Baluba were past masters in the construction of elephant traps that were so expertly camouflaged as to be invisible from the air. Some of these traps, dug into the center of the track, were big enough to accommodate a five-ton truck and impossible to spot from the road until it was too late to avoid them.

The dawn raid on Kasongo proved abortive and yielded one prisoner only, the man in the blue shirt and trousers we had seen from the air. He turned out to be a deaf mute. That presumably explained his lack of emotion when we flew over him recently. I then ordered the infantry company to patrol the hinterland on foot, to find the new villages which air had told us had been built deep in the bush, miles from the road, and to bring in as many prisoners as they could.

The main column sped on for Mwenge. The *groupe mobile* had abandoned all pretense at caution and was racing for the town, putting their trust in speed and a surprise attack. It was a gamble that did not come off. Disaster hit them before they had traveled many kilometers. The lead jeep, which was lightly armored, ran straight into an elephant trap and dropped about fifteen feet into a pit spiked with hundreds of sharpened bamboo stakes, seriously wounding the driver, an Italian mercenary officer, and two men. A bamboo stake had penetrated the officer's chest and ruptured his spleen. The trap itself was undefended but it took over two hours to extricate the vehicle and the wounded men. The pain the lieutenant suffered must have been excruciating but he was conscious right through it to the end. He had lost a considerable quantity of blood and our only hope of saving him was to get him back to Kiambi as soon as we could. I sent him off with an escort but he died on the way. His men told me later that the jolting of the truck on the rough track had finally proved too much for him.

Strangely enough I had been talking with this officer only the day before and had noticed that he always traveled with two spare wheels in his jeep. He said he was taking no chances in this neck of the woods. A fellow countryman of his had been on patrol in the Manono area some weeks previously, had had a puncture, and then another, and was marooned in the bush miles from any help. While the other truck in the patrol went for assistance his friend's group was attacked by the Jeunesse, overwhelmed, and speared to death.

I examined the construction of the elephant trap. It had been made with fiendish cunning. Once the hole had been dug, and this must have been a major engineering feat, it had been covered over with bamboo poles stretching from one side of the hole to the other. These surface poles were supported from below with vertical ones. Over the top they had placed several lengths of coconut matting covered with soil a few inches deep, which made it indistinguishable from the road. A single tire had then been rolled twice over the soil leaving a track which made it look as though a vehicle had passed over it recently. The bottom of the pit was embedded with sharpened bamboo stakes, some of them three or four feet long. They had carried the spoil from the hole a good distance away and that was probably why traps like these were so difficult to detect from the air.

During the time it took to rescue the crew of the jeep and recover the vehicle the drums began to beat. Once again the jungle telegraph was at work in its mysterious way and any hope we had of reaching Mwenge now with total surprise was gone. The chances of capturing a large number of prisoners in that town were nil. I decided to return to my headquarters at the iron bridge while the *groupe mobile* was to continue with its operation. They returned late that evening with about eighty prisoners, the majority of whom they had captured in the smaller villages surrounding Mwenge. Mwenge itself was abandoned by the time they got there. This was bad luck but I was confident the prisoners they had brought back, plus those the Katangese infantry had brought in from the hinterland behind Kasongo, would be enough to give us the answer to those three vital questions: what happened to Simon and Ted on May 7, who killed them, and where?

The next morning I witnessed an incident that, for sheer callous brutality, would be hard to equal. The hundred or so Baluba prisoners were now under the command of a Katangese lieutenant named Kitenge George. He always announced himself in this back to front fashion, surname first, which is the normal thing in the Congo, as it is in some European countries. Lieutenant Kitenge had lately returned from the Military College in Brussels and had a head stuffed full with military lore but very little else it would seem. I was now to discover that underneath his veneer of civilization he was nothing but an unthinking savage.

It was time to transport the prisoners to our base at Kiambi for further interrogation. The majority of them were roped together in a compound by the bridge and were now untied so that they could be herded into the backs of trucks. But before that could happen Kitenge George intended to have some fun. He shouted an order to his men who began at once to chivy the prisoners into a group facing down the track, using the butt ends of their rifles with enthusiasm. He then lined up his Katangese company in two ranks, between the trucks and the prisoners. On his command the soldiers faced each other, an arm's length apart. When Kitenge blew his whistle the prisoners were to run, one at a time, through this narrow corridor of men and then jump into the nearest truck standing with its tailgate down, about twenty yards beyond the last soldier . . . if they could.

The first man to run the gauntlet was an agile youngster who flew down the track, fending off blows and kicks from both sides all the way down the tunnel, amid shouts and screams of laughter from the soldiers. They were having fun. He made it about halfway. A rifle butt in the neck floored him. As soon as he was down heavy boots thudded into him. He was left where he lay, motionless. The whistle blew again and the second man raced down the track. His chances of reaching the safety of the truck were nil. The blood lust of the soldiers was running high. Now a crescendo of animal-like yelps accompanied the dull thud of boots and rifle butts on naked bodies as, one by one, the prisoners hit the ground and lay there, many of them unconscious.

None of the first ten made it to the truck. A *madala*, an old man, declined to take part in the little game and walked slowly and with incredible dignity toward the soldiers, his head held high. For a moment they did not know how to deal with him, but the indecision lasted less than fifteen seconds. He was clubbed to the ground. Then a small slender boy, not waiting for the whistle, flew down the track with the speed and agility of a small deer. Just as it looked as though he was going to make it he was felled, staggered to his feet, darted through the ranks and went like the clappers of hell for the safety of the bush, jinking like a bushbuck from side to side as he ran. A burst of automatic fire from Kitenge George hit him as he looked back. I was close enough to see the look of reproach in his eyes as he died. "Why did you have to do that?" he seemed to say.

Whatever this nonsense was meant to be it had gone too far. I gave an order to Kitenge to stop it at once. He ignored it and me. He gave me a look as though to say, "Who the hell are you anyway?" I soon told him. He pretended he could not understand a simple order in French and turned his back on me. I was livid with anger. But Lambrette intervened and took a more practical line. "Four more and then call it a day," he suggested to Kitenge, in Swahili, and that was exactly what Kitenge did.

Not one prisoner made it to the truck without a bloody beating. The soldiers lifted them off the ground and threw their inert bodies into the camions like so many sides of beef. It came as a profound shock to me that human beings could behave in this barbaric way, but I had to remind myself that this was a matter of tribal custom and tradition. Hadn't I told my own officers time and again that we were not here to pass judgment on the Katangese or the Baluba and their traditional ways of making war? Wasn't this exactly what I had warned them against? But here I was doing just that. The ill treatment and torture of prisoners was a normal part of tribal warfare, and had been going on for centuries. Nothing I was going to do or say would make the slightest difference. It would still go on. But was that an excuse for condoning it?

Later in the day it was reported to me that Kitenge had shot two of the prisoners after interrogation, *pour encourager les autres*, I supposed. I made sure Lambrette sent in a report to Etat Major about the incident at the end of the operation but to my knowledge nothing was ever done about it. We were really in the heart of darkness. Here a human life counted for practically nothing. It evoked memories of what Vachel Lindsay, the poet, had written: Then I heard the boom of the blood-lust song /And a thigh-bone beating on a tin-pan gong.

It was barbarity in its most basic form, but barbarity with a subtle difference. Sir Richard Burton, the famous explorer, was right when he said mere barbarism rarely disgusts: it is the unnatural union of civilization with savagery that makes the gorge rise. The incongruities are not grotesque enough to be amusing; they are merely ugly and painful.

The interrogation of the prisoners began. After two days some hard information emerged, most of it based on hearsay; however, a common thread appeared to run through it all. It seemed highly probable that Simon and Ted had arrived at Kalamata before noon on May 7. They drove their jeep to the chief's hut and approached the chief as friends. Simon had asked in Swahili if they were friendly with Mr. Tshombe. Plainly he could have had no idea where he was. They had then been seized, taken to Kasongo, and killed by the Jeunesse at about three that afternoon. The sultan of Kalamata was a man named M'Buyu Kepo. It was thought he had ordered the capture and killing of the two men. Nobody knew where M'Buyu Kepo was now. After the killings the people of Kalamata, Kiungu, and all the villages around feared reprisals from the Katangese Army and disappeared into the bush, abandoning their villages.

This general story seemed to me to have the ring of truth about it, but Lambrette said he was not entirely convinced. There were no eyewitnesses after all, it was all hearsay, and he would like to take the matter further. He had contacts among some friendly Baluba who were still living in the *cité* in Manono and he would offer a reward for information. He had no doubt that he would get at the truth finally, but it would take time. He agreed that we would never see Simon or Ted again. When I asked him what he thought had happened between the time when they were first taken prisoner before noon and three in the afternoon when they were killed he said there were some things in the Katanga it would be wiser not to inquire into too deeply.

We fell back on Kalamata for the last time. At long last it seemed to have yielded up its secrets. Personally I had no doubt that the sultan was guilty of murdering the two men and of who knew what else besides. As a punishment I ordered the village to be burned. The Katangese soldiers put their torches to the huts with enthusiasm. A strong breeze fanned the flames as they raced from hut to hut. The thatch began to crackle and spit and the air above the village blackened to hide the sun. In no time a huge pall of smoke hung above it and began to rise high into the air, visible for miles around. Glowing hot wisps of burnt thatch floated to the ground like a fall of black snow, leaving sooty marks on everything it touched. The heat forced me back into the long grass to windward of the burning village where I watched the huts slowly collapse and disappear.

My thoughts were deep on Simon and Ted and the horror of their last minutes of life in this accursed village. A Belgian mercenary chose this inauspicious minute to ask me in a surly manner if I appreciated the enormity of the punishment I was imposing on the Baluba. There were over five hundred huts here, he said, and when the war was over the villagers of Kalamata would want to return to occupy them again. To burn their village was a monstrous thing. I told him not to interfere, I was in command and this was my judgment, a collective punishment for the murder of my two men, probably after ritual torture if my information was anything to go by. He began to give me the benefit of his opinions. Finally I lost my temper and said, "Bugger off quick! Don't give me any more of that damned nonsense or I'll have you burned at the same time, you stupid bastard!" The absurd threat frightened the life out of him and I saw him no more. He had something to talk about when he got back to Brussels, I've no doubt.

I spent two nights and two days at Manono where the interrogation of the prisoners continued. I filed my report and handed back the patrol to Captain Protin. I was free to return to Elizabethville whenever I wished.

It was the end of the road.

I decided to get back to Elizabethville by truck rather than wait for the next plane, which was not due for four days. My route passed through the straggling town of Bunkeya, the ancient capital of the Bayeke. The ghosts of the past seemed to whisper to me as I drove slowly through the sandy main street on my way south to Jadotville. An enormous crowd thronged the road bringing all traffic to a standstill. It was some sort of wedding procession. When I eventually reached the front of it I saw the bridegroom wheeling his bride in all her regalia on the handlebars of his bicycle, presumably to some sort of celebration—the wedding reception no doubt. They had just been married at the Roman Catholic Church nearby. There was happiness and laughter in the air.

It all seemed so incongruous and improbable. Was this really Bunkeya, the famous capital city of the Bayeke, the fiercest warrior tribe in Katanga of yesteryear, whose very name had been a byword for terror in the Congo as recently as the end of the last century? Was this really where the infamous M'Siri, King of Katanga, had been killed by Captain Bodson, a Belgian officer in Captain William Stairs' expedition of 1891? Was this where the Belgians had cut off the old tyrant's head and carried it away in a paraffin tin for subsequent display so that no one could dispute his death? And could it only have been a mere three score years and ten, one man's lifetime, since all this had happened—since Katanga, the richest mineral country in the world, passed into the personal possession of King Leopold II of the Belgians, there to form part of his private domain, the Congo, the largest piece of real estate ever to be owned by one man in all of history, exceeding in extent one million square miles? It was, of course. And for my further amazement I had to remind myself of the irrefutable fact that M'Siri's grandson was none other than Godefroid Munongo, Minister of the Interior in the Independent State of Katanga, one of its leading and most respected statesmen. Evolution. What else?

I called on Major Falques on my way through Jadotville as a matter of courtesy and reported to him on the patrol. He showed no emotion. It was precisely what he had expected. Just as I was about to leave he handed me a letter from Etat Major with a glint of amusement in his eye. It was addressed to me personally. I was called upon to account for two million Katangese francs worth of stores, etc., missing from the convoy I had escorted to Nyunzu. Offer to pay one hundred francs a month and see what they say, he said with glee.

I hurried back to Elizabethville to resume my extraordinary honeymoon and to bring Speedy Donaldson up to date with my news. The marble floors and crystal chandeliers of the Leo Deux brought me back with a jolt to the so-called civilized world we live in. Phyllis was looking delectable in the midst of a party of journalists who were doing their best to ignore the rifle fire that was erupting spasmodically quite near the hotel, most of it from the direction of the newly erected Baluba refugee camp. From time to time their laughter was interrupted by the ominous stutter of machine gun fire, a lot nearer.

She introduced me to a tall young man, annoyingly good looking, drat him.

"This is Harry Byrnes," she said. "He's a correspondent for one of the British newspapers. We met in rather a thrilling way last night. As I was coming down for dinner someone fired some bullets into the windows on the first floor. I was so frightened I dashed into the nearest room and flung myself under the bed for protection."

I wasn't sure I liked the way the story was going.

"And then?"

"Why," she said, rather pleased with herself, "that's where I met Harry. He was under the bed already!"

Well, now that I had another look at him, he didn't seem such a bad chap after all.

Meanwhile in the foyer of the Leo Deux an exceptionally handsome Frenchman, a correspondent for one of the French newspapers, was having problems reaching his head office in Paris. Finally he managed to get through. Delicately removing an amber cigarette holder from his mouth he tapped away the ash. Then, leaning nonchalantly across the reception desk, he spoke languidly into the mouthpiece, just as a burst of machine gun fire erupted in the street outside.

"*Mais oui, mon vieux*, but yes, yes, old chum," he agreed, "you're right. It is. It's hell here, absolute hell. No, no, please not to worry about me—all part of the job. Of course I'll ring again, same time tomorrow—that is, if they don't get me in the meantime." He replaced the receiver, adjusted his bow tie, and flicked a speck of dust from the sleeve of his immaculate dinner jacket.

A moment later a glamorous and sophisticated lady swept down the marble stairs, one arm extended, to join him. She wore a black evening gown cut imprudently low at the bosom, a red hibiscus in her upswept hair, another strategically placed on her frontispiece, or whatever. He bowed and kissed her hand gently by way of salute, after which the elegant pair swept out to a waiting taxi followed by a flutter of mild applause from us all. War is hell.

I met Speedy for the last time and gave him a full report on the second phase of the operation. He listened intently without saying a word. I noticed with dismay that he had withdrawn once more into his shell. Gone was the easy camaraderie we had established in the bush while on patrol. That was another world. Pity. He thanked me briefly for my assistance and said he had resigned himself to the facts. Without any sign of emotion he said he now accepted that Simon was dead. He was about to leave for the airport and I went with him to a taxi. We shook hands. Even though we were poles apart in our way of life, and probably in almost everything else, I had developed something amounting to affection for him. This might have developed into friendship in time if he had permitted it. But it was not to be. Sadly for me he reduced everything to the mundane in one banal stroke.

"By the way," he said, "I expect you have been put to some expense over this matter. Well, in due course I expect Mr. Tshombe's government will send me the indemnity I am entitled to as a result of Simon's death. When that happens you can send me a note of your expenditure if you wish."

I made no comment, then or later, but I never lost my admiration for a man who could accept a blow of fate as cruel as this without a murmur of self-pity.

About a year later I met Mr. Donaldson again. He explained that it was necessary for him to apply to the Supreme Court in South Africa for an assumption of Simon's death, in order to wind up Simon's considerable estate. A statement of the circumstances leading to his death was required from me under oath. Would I please attend at his lawyer's office for this purpose? I said I would and did. It was the last time I ever saw Mr. Donaldson.

And that was the end of the affair as far as I was concerned, or would have been had it not been for an extraordinary twist of fate. Three years later, in 1964, I was once more in Katanga. This time I was in command of a unit of mercenary soldiers that I had named 5 Commando. This unit had been raised by order of the government of the Democratic Republic of the Congo in Leopoldville to assist the Congolese National Army put down a communist-inspired rebellion, which had broken out in the northeastern corner of the Congo in the province of Orientale. The rebels had already overrun two-thirds of the Congo with the speed and ferocity of a bush fire, and were at that very moment holding hostage more than 125 Europeans and Americans whom they threatened to put to death if Stanleyville, the headquarters of the insurrection, was attacked by the Congolese army. In October of that year 5 Commando was in training at Kamina base in Katanga, preparing to help the Congolese National Army recapture Stanleyville.*

During the three years that had passed since I was in Katanga with 4 Commando, tribal allegiances, which formed part of the vicissitudes of Congolese politics at that time, had changed drastically. Incredible as it may have seemed, the Baluba were now allies of the Congolese government and no longer the enemy as in 1961! This was to have consequences I could never have foreseen.

One day I was visited at Kamina by Major André Protin, now officer commanding the Manono district. He handed me a report he had received a few days earlier from Adjudant Edouard Lambrette, who was serving under him once again. The letter was written from Piana Mwanga. It said:

Mon Major,
On 13 October 1964 I completed a patrol to Kalamata. I brought back from the village the uncle of one of the authors of the assassination of two South Africans in 1960 *[sic]*. That is to say the uncle of M'Buyu Kepo. The latter has built his own village 1 km from Kalamata, in the direction Kiambi. The village of

*See *Congo Mercenary* by Mike Hoare.

Kalamata no longer exists. That one has been completely burned down.
I have interrogated M'Buyu Kepo's uncle who is named Kabila-Mungelele, date of birth 1910, of the village of Kalamata.

Q. Who are you?
A. The uncle of M'Buyu Kepo.

Q. Where do you live?
A. At M'Buyu Kepo's village, 1 km from Kalamata.

Q. Who killed the two Europeans in 1960?
A. M'Buyu Kepo, with the aid of the new sultan of Kalamata named Kiungu-Kioma.

Q. Where were they killed?
A. They were killed at the village of Kasongo.

Q. Where were they stopped?
A. At the bridge over the Lubalashi. It spans this river.

Q. Were they tortured? By whom and where?
A. They were tortured by M'Buyu Kepo, Kiungu-Kioma, and the chief of Kasongo.

Q. Was the chief of Kasongo an accomplice?
A. Yes, and the friend of M'Buyu Kepo.

Q. What is the name of the chief of the village of Kasongo?
A. He is called Kasongo.

Q. Where were the bodies hidden?
A. I heard it said that they were buried opposite the village of Kasongo, very near the right-hand side of the road in the direction of Baudouinville.

Q. Who took their guns?
A. M'Buyu Kepo took the two guns and Kiungu-Kioma the revolver.

Q. Who took their clothes and other things?
A. M'Buyu Kepo.

Q. Who took the jeep?
A. M'Buyu Kepo.

Q. Where was the jeep hidden?
A. On the road from Kashimba, by the side of the village.

Q. Who drove the jeep?
A. The Jeunesse of M'Buyu Kepo.

Q. Give me the names of several of the participants in the murder.
A. Uma Lukolomona, Mkulu Muke, Mwamba Muke.

Q. Who was the chief witch doctor in 1960 of the region?
A. It was a woman of the village of Mutumbi named Ilunga Walekwa.

The Adjudant ended by requesting permission to make further inquiries.

The Major now asked me if I could attach one of my officers to his headquarters in order to go further into the matter and perhaps to try to recover the bodies. He said he had already informed the British Consul in Elizabethville. I replied that just at this moment we were about to take part in the operation against Stanleyville and I regretted I could not spare an officer for this purpose. He said he planned to convene a court of inquiry to go thoroughly into the affair, and he would let me know how things turned out in due course.

Another year passed and now my headquarters was in Albertville on the shores of Lake Tanganyika. One day I was delighted to receive a personal visit from Major Protin who was still commanding the Manono district. He handed me a file marked "Affaire Donaldson et MacKay."

That file, yellowed and worn with the passage of time, lies before me as I write these words. It contains conclusive evidence from a number of eyewitnesses that Simon Donaldson and Ted MacKay were done to death by the Baluba Jeunesse on May 7, 1961, after having been ritually tortured. I end by recording the evidence of two of the eyewitnesses. Some of the others are too horrible to relate.

Deposition of eyewitness Kakudji Mulenda, born in 1940, at Kalamata.

Q. Kabila Mengelele accuses you of having taken part in the murder of two Europeans in 1961.

A. I did nothing to them but I was present.

Q. Do you know those who took part in this affair?

A. M'Buyu Kepo, Uma Lukolomona, Nkulu Moke, Nkulu Vincent, Chief Kasongo Kamulumbi, a soldier of the Congolese Army named Senga Waboko, Umba Oswald, the Sultan Kyungu Kaniama, Banza Manuel, Kmona Kimiama, Kinengo Ilunga, Mwamba Bruxelles, Mwilambwe Mukundji.

Q. Where were they stopped?

A. At the bridge which spans the River Lubalashi.

Q. Where did they take their arms from them?

A. At the village of Kasongo.

Q. Who took them?

A. M'Buyu Kepo and Senga Waboka.

Q. Where were you precisely at this moment?

A. Round about the two whites whom we had encircled.

Q. Did they resist?

A. No, because we were too numerous.

Q. What time was it when they were stopped?

A. About eleven o'clock, twelve o'clock.

Q. Where were they taken?

A. To the village of Kasongo.

Q. With the agreement of chief Kasongo Kamulumbi?

A. Yes.

Q. Was chief Kasongo an accomplice?

A. Yes. He was one of those who fired on the two whites.

Q. Were they tortured? By whom?

A. Yes. By chief Kasongo, M'Buyu Kepo, and Senga Waboka, Uma Lukolomona, Banza Manuel, Nkulu Vincent.

Q. How?

A. They beat them a lot because both of them were crying.

Q. At what time did they kill them?

A. About fifteen hours.

Q. Who killed the first white man?
A. It was a soldier from the Congolese Army, Senga Wa-boka, who fired the first shots at the first white man, two bullets in the chest; and it was M'Buyu Kepo who finished off the first white man with a bullet in the head.

Q. Who killed the second white man?
A. It was Kasongo Kamulumbi who fired first on the second white man, one bullet in the chest; and after that Kyungu Kanamia finished him off with two bullets, one in the head and the other in the chest.

Q. Did they die at once?
A. Yes.

Q. What did you do then?
A. We buried them immediately.

Q. Where?
A. Between the bridge over the Lubalashi and the village, on the right-hand side of the road, behind the bridge.

Q. Do you know the place, could you show it to me?
A. Yes, roughly, because it is already a long time ago.

Q. Who took the weapons?
A. M'Buyu Kepo took the two rifles and Chief Kasongo Kamulumbi the two revolvers.

Q. Are you sure that there were two revolvers?
A. Yes, I saw them myself.

Q. Who took the jeep?
A. M'Buyu Kepo.

Q. Who took their personal belongings?
A. The chiefs shared them between themselves.

Q. Where did they hide the jeep?
A. By the side of the village of Lubamba on the right of the road from Kashimba.

Q. Who drove the jeep.
A. Umba Oswald, a former driver of Mr. Antoniou Kyr-
iacos, a Manono businessman.

Q. Where are the weapons?
A. They were taken by the Congolese National Army.

Signed Kakudji Mulenda, born in 1940. I certify that I have
replied without constraint to the questions put to me and
to the best of my ability.

Another eyewitness, Uma Locolomona, born in 1940 at Kalamata,
and one of those accused of the murder, also answered questions but
his answers differed in some respects:

Q. At what hour were they stopped?
A. About ten hours.

Q. Did they resist?
A. No.

Q. Did the Europeans give up their arms themselves?
A. Yes, they gave them up voluntarily.

Q. To whom did they give their arms?
A. To chief Kasongo Kamulumbi.

Q. Why, in order to show they were friends?
A. Yes.

Q. What did they do to them?
A. They tortured them.

Q. What time were they killed?
A. About twelve hours.

Q. Who fired on the older of the two white men?
A. Kyungu Kiniama fired twice and M'Buyu Kepo once.

Q. Did chief Kasongo fire on the two white men?
A. Yes, two shots from a poupou. (A shot gun.)

There are two words in the interrogation above that will haunt
me for the rest of my days. They are *ils pleuraient*—they were crying.

I have never forgotten Simon and Ted and I often pray for the repose of their souls. Have mercy on them, O Lord. Let them take refuge in the shadow of your wings now that the disaster has passed.

About the Author

Mike Hoare was born in India of Irish parents, spent some of his early days in Ireland, and was educated in England. He served in the British Army in the U.K., India, and Burma for seven years and was discharged with the rank of major. After World War II he qualified in London as a chartered accountant and emigrated to South Africa where he began his own safari business. He traveled extensively in Africa south of the Sahara. He commanded a unit of mercenary soldiers in Katanga in 1961 and another in the Congo in 1964 and 1965. After working as an accountant in the Far East he sailed his own 100-ton Baltic trader around the Mediterranean Sea for three years with his family as crew. As a result of his experiences in the Congo he is a confirmed anticommunist. In 1981 he led an abortive coup against the Marxist government of the Seychelles, as a result of which he was sentenced to a term of imprisonment in a South African jail. On his release he undertook a pilgrimage on foot from Le Puy in France to Santiago de Compostela in Spain with his two student sons, both of whom are studying in the USA. They covered a distance of over 500 miles. He says his sons have never forgiven him. In the early sixties Colonel Hoare saw a great future for properly disciplined units of mercenary soldiers who could have been employed in support of the armies of newly formed African countries. He regrets that this opportunity vanished largely as a result of bad behavior on the part of some mercenary soldiers themselves, the resultant bad press, and grossly distorted stories told about their activities. He is happily married.